MUSIC QUICKENS TIME

MUSIC QUICKENS TIME

DANIEL BARENBOIM

Edited by Elena Cheah

VERSO

London • New York

This paperback edition published by Verso 2009
US edition first published by Verso 2008
© Daniel Barenboim 2008
© Giangiacomo Feltrinelli Editore, Milano 2007

1 3 5 7 9 10 8 6 4 2

Verso
UK: 6 Meard Street, London W1F 0EG
US: 20 Jay Street, Suite 1010, Brooklyn, NY 11201
www.versobooks.com

Verso is the imprint of New Left Books

ISBN-13: 978-1-84467-402-2

British Library Cataloguing in Publication Data
A catalogue record for this book is available from the British Library

Library of Congress Cataloging-in-Publication Data
A catalog record for this book is available from the Library of Congress

Typeset in Fournier by Hewer Text UK Ltd, Edinburgh
Printed in the USA by Maple Vail

To the musicians of the West-Eastern Divan Orchestra

Contents

Part One

The Power of Music

Prelude

The beginning of a concert is more privileged than the beginning of a book. One could say that sound itself is more privileged than words. A book is full of the same words that are used every day, day after day, to explain, describe, demand, argue, beg, enthuse, tell the truth and lie. Our thoughts take shape in words; therefore, the words on the page must compete with the words in our minds. Music has a much larger world of associations at its disposal precisely because of its ambivalent nature; it is both inside and outside the world.

In today's world, music has a cacophonous omnipresence in restaurants, airplanes and the like, but it is precisely this omnipresence that represents the greatest hindrance to the integration of music into our society. No school would eliminate the study of language, mathematics, or history from its curriculum, yet the study of music, which encompasses so many aspects of these fields and can even contribute to a better understanding of them, is often entirely ignored.

This is not a book for musicians, nor is it one for non-musicians, but rather for the curious mind that wishes to discover the parallels between music and life and the wisdom that becomes audible to the thinking ear. This is not a privilege reserved for highly talented musicians who receive musical training from a very early age, nor is it an ivory tower, an exclusive luxury for the wealthy; I would contend that it is a basic necessity to develop the intelligence of the ear. As I will explain in the chapter "Listening and Hearing," we can learn a great deal for life from the structures, principles and laws inherent in music, whether these are experienced by the listener or the performer.

Many of the topics I discuss in this book are ones that have occupied my thoughts for decades, and are the result of nearly sixty years of performance, instruction and contemplation. In my first book, *A Life in Music*, which has an autobiographical thread without being an autobiography, I began to touch on these subjects. In the book I wrote with Edward Said, *Parallels and Paradoxes*, we explored the relationships between music and society. When I was invited to deliver the Norton lectures at Harvard University in the autumn of 2006, I naturally seized the opportunity to develop my ideas on the connections between music and life more extensively, and this book is a further development of these thoughts.

1

Sound and Thought

I firmly believe that it is impossible to speak about music. There have been many definitions of music which have, in fact, merely described a subjective reaction to it. The only really precise and objective definition for me is by Ferruccio Busoni, the great Italian pianist and composer, who said that music is sonorous air. It says everything and nothing at the same time. Schopenhauer, on the other hand, saw in music an idea of the world. In music, as in life, it is really only possible to speak about our own reactions and perceptions. If I attempt to speak about music, it is because the impossible has always attracted me more than the difficult. If there is some sense behind this, to attempt the impossible is, by definition, an adventure and gives me a feeling of activity, which I find highly attractive. It has the added advantage that failure is not only tolerated but expected. I will therefore attempt the impossible and try to draw some connections between the inexpressible content of music and the inexpressible content of life.

Isn't music, after all, just a collection of beautiful sounds? John Locke wrote in his—in many ways—very forward-looking treatise, "Some Thoughts Concerning Education," published in 1692, that "Musick is thought to have some affinity with dancing, and a good hand upon some instruments is by many people mightily valued. But it wastes so much of a young man's time to gain but a moderate skill in it; and engages often in such odd company, that many think it much better spared: and I have amongst men of parts and business so seldom heard any one commended or esteemed for having an excellency in musick, that amongst all those things that ever came into the list of accomplishments, I think I may give it the last place." Today, music still often takes the last place in our own thoughts concerning education. Is music really more than something very agreeable or exciting to listen to—something that, through its sheer power and eloquence, gives us formidable tools with which we can forget our existence and the chores of daily life? Millions of people, of course, like to come home after a long day at work, put on some music and forget all the problems of the day. I contend, however, that music also gives us another far more valuable tool, with which we can learn about ourselves, about our society, about politics—in short, about the human being. Aristotle, preceding John Locke by nearly two thousand years, held music in higher esteem, deeming it a valuable contribution to the education of the young: "But music is pursued, not only as an alleviation of past toil, but also as providing recreation. And who can say whether, having this use, it may not also have a nobler one? . . . Rhythm and melody supply imitations of anger and gentleness, and also of courage and temperance, and of all the qualities contrary to these, and of the other qualities of character, which hardly fall short of the actual affections, as we know from our own experience, for in listening to such strains our souls undergo a change . . . Enough has been said to show that music has a power of forming the character, and should therefore be introduced into the education of the young."[1]

Let us first look at the physical phenomenon that allows us to experience a piece of music, which is sound. Here we encounter one of the great difficulties in defining music: music expresses itself through sound, but sound in itself is not yet music—it is merely the means by which the message of music or its content is transmitted. When describing sound, very often we speak in terms of color: a bright sound or a dark sound. This is very subjective; what is dark for one is light for the other and vice versa. There are other elements of sound, however, which are not subjective. Sound is a physical reality that can and should be observed objectively. When doing so, we notice that it disappears as it stops; it is ephemeral. It is not an object, such as a chair, which you can leave in an empty room and return later to find it still there, just as you left it. Sound does not remain in this world; it evaporates into silence.

Sound is not independent—it does not exist by itself, but has a permanent, constant and unavoidable relationship to silence. In this context the first note is not the beginning, but comes out of the silence that precedes it. If sound stands in relation to silence, what kind of relationship is it? Does sound dominate silence, or does silence dominate sound? After careful observation, we notice that the relationship between sound and silence is the equivalent of the relationship between a physical object and the force of gravity. An object that is lifted from the ground demands a certain amount of energy to keep it at the height to which it has been raised. Unless one provides additional energy, the object will fall to the ground, obeying the laws of gravity. In much the same way, unless sound is sustained, it is driven to silence. The musician who produces a sound literally brings it into the physical world. Furthermore, unless he provides added energy, the sound will die. This is the lifespan of a single note—it is finite. The terminology is plain: the note dies. And here we might have the first clear indication of content in music: the disappearance of sound by its transformation into silence is the definition of its being limited in time.

Some instruments, particularly percussion instruments, including the piano, produce sounds that we refer to as having a real-life duration; in other words, after the sound is produced, it immediately begins to decay. With others, such as stringed instruments, there are ways to sustain the sound longer than that of a percussion instrument: for example, by changing the direction of the bow and making the change smooth enough so that it becomes inaudible. Sustaining the sound is in any case an act of defiance against the pull of silence, which attempts to limit the length of the sound.

Let us examine the different possibilities presented by the beginning of sound. If there is total silence before the beginning, we start a piece of music that either interrupts the silence or evolves out of it. The sound that interrupts the silence represents an alteration of an existing situation, whereas the sound evolving out of the silence is a gradual alteration of the existing situation. In philosophical language, one could call this the difference between being and becoming. The opening of Beethoven's Pathétique Sonata, Op. 13,[2] is an obvious case of the interruption of silence. The very definite chord interrupts the silence and the music begins. The prelude to *Tristan und Isolde* is an obvious example of the sound evolving out of silence.[3]

The music does not begin with the move from the initial A to the F, but from the silence to the A. Or, in Beethoven's Piano Sonata Op. 109,[4] one has the feeling that the music began earlier—it is as if one steps onto a train that is by now in motion. The music must already exist in the mind of the pianist, so that when he plays, he creates an impression that he joins what has been in existence, albeit not in the physical world. In the Pathétique Sonata the accent on the first note makes a very definite break with silence. In Op. 109 it is imperative not to start with an accent on the first note, because the accent by definition would interrupt the silence.

The last sound is not the end of the music. If the first note is related to the silence that precedes it, then the last note must be related to the silence that follows it. This is why it is so disruptive when an enthusiastic audience applauds before the final sound has died away, because there is one last moment of expressivity, which is precisely the relationship between the end of the sound and the beginning of the silence that follows it. In this respect music is a mirror of life, because both start and end in nothing. Furthermore, when playing music it is possible to achieve a unique state of peace, partly due to the fact that one can control, through sound, the relationship between life and death, a power that obviously is not bestowed upon human beings in life. Since every note produced by a human being has a human quality, there is a feeling of death with the end of each one, and through that experience there is a transcendence of all the emotions that these notes can have in their short lives; in a way one is in direct contact with timelessness. When I finish playing one of the books of *The Well-Tempered Clavier* in one evening, I have the feeling that this is actually much longer than my real life, that I have been on a journey through history, one that begins and ends in silence.

One way of preparing silence is to create a tremendous amount of tension preceding it, so that the silence arrives only after the absolute height of intensity and volume has been reached. Another way of approaching silence entails a gradual diminution of sound, letting the music become so soft that the next possible step can only be silence. Silence, in other words, can be louder than the maximum and softer than the minimum. Total silence exists, of course, also within a composition. It is temporary death, followed by the ability to revive, to begin life anew. In this way music is more than a mirror of life; it is enriched by the metaphysical dimension of sound, which gives it the possibility to transcend physical, human limitations. In the world of sound, even death is not necessarily final.

It is obvious that if a sound has a beginning and a duration, it also has an end, whether dying or giving way to the next note. Notes that follow each other operate clearly within the inevitable passage of time. Expressiveness in music comes from linking the notes, what we call in Italian *legato*, which means nothing other than bound. This dictates that the notes cannot be allowed to develop their natural egos, becoming so dominant that they overshadow the preceding one. Each note must be aware of itself but also of its own boundaries; the same rules that apply to individuals in society apply to notes in music as well. When one plays five legato notes, each fights against the power of silence that wants to take its life, and therefore stands in relation to the notes that precede and follow it. Each note cannot be self-assertive, wanting to be louder than the notes preceding it; if it did, it would defy the nature of the phrase to which it belongs. A musician must possess the capacity to group notes. This very simple fact has taught me the relationship between an individual and a group. It is necessary for the human being to contribute to society in a very individual way; this makes the whole much larger than the sum of its parts. Individuality and collectivism need not be mutually exclusive; in fact, together they are capable of enhancing human existence.

The content of music can only be articulated through sound. As we have already seen, any verbalization is nothing but a description of our subjective—maybe even haphazard—reaction to the music. But the fact that the content of music cannot be articulated in words does not, of course, mean that it has no content; if that were the case, musical performances would be totally unnecessary and it would be unthinkable to be interested in composers such as Bach who lived several centuries ago. Nevertheless, we must never stop asking ourselves what exactly the content of music is, this intangible substance that is expressible only through sound. It cannot be defined as having merely a mathematical, a poetic, or a sensual content. It is all those things and much more. It has to do with the condition of being human, since the music is written and performed by human beings who express their innermost thoughts, feelings, impressions and observations. This is true of all music regardless of the period in which composers lived and the obvious stylistic differences between them. For example, three hundred years separate Bach and Boulez, yet both created worlds which we, as performers and listeners, render contemporary. The condition of being human can obviously be as large or as small as the human being chooses it to be, and one could say the same of composition itself. The renowned conductor Sergiu Celibidache said that music does not become something, but that something may become music. He meant that the difference between sound—just pure sound or a collection of sounds—and music is that, when one makes music, all the elements have to be integrated into an organic whole. There are no independent elements in music— rhythm is not independent of melody, melody is obviously not independent of harmony and not even tempo is an independent phenomenon. We tend to think that because some composers give us metronome markings, all we have to do is to try to squeeze all the notes and their expression into a certain speed, forgetting that one does not actually hear tempo, one only hears the music at a given speed. If the tempo is too fast, the content is incomprehensible because of the performer's inability to play all the notes clearly or the listener's inability to grasp them; if the tempo is too slow it is equally incomprehensible, because neither the performer nor the listener is able to perceive all the relationships between the notes.

Richard Wagner wrote in his 1869 treatise *On Conducting* that *"the right comprehension of the melos is the sole guide to the right tempo*; these two things are inseparable: the one implies and qualifies the other. As a proof of my assertion that the majority of performances of instrumental music with us are faulty it is sufficient to point out that *our conductors so frequently fail to find the true tempo because they are ignorant of singing."* Describing the difference between the character of the Adagio and the Allegro movements in Beethoven symphonies, he continues, "the slow emanations of pure tone on the one hand [in reference to the Adagio], and the most rapid figurated movement on the other [in the Allegro], are subject to ideal limits only, and in both directions the law of beauty is the sole measure of what is possible. The law of beauty establishes the point of contact at which the opposite extremes tend to meet and to unite."

Interestingly, Wagner speaks not of melody but of the melos. The word "melos" makes its first appearance in the poetry of the Archilochos of Paros in the seventh century BC; there it refers to a choral song. Later Plato defined melos as the synthesis of word, tonality and rhythm, whereas Aristotle's definition was closer to our own understanding of melody. In *Politics* he names three different varieties of *mele*: the ethical, the practical, and the ecstatic.[5] Wagner teaches us that the melos is the sole criterion for choosing the right tempo, which means that the decision about the correct tempo is not dependent on an outside factor such as the metronome and, just as important, that it is the last decision a musician should take. Only after observation of all the elements inherent in the music's content can he determine the speed with which these can be expressed. Therefore, a decision taken too early makes one a slave of the tempo, whereas a decision taken at the end of the learning process takes all factors into consideration. Like so many things in life, the rightness of a decision is inevitably linked to the moment in which it is made.

The understanding of the interdependence of different elements in music requires an understanding of the relationship between space and time, or, in other words, the relationship between subject matter and speed. Speed, or tempo, which may seem to be outside the music itself, is also not independent. The relationship between the texture and the volume of the sound on the one hand and the audible transparency of the music on the other determines the correct speed. In tonal music, to explain the system of music used in between 1600–1900 and in most of today's popular music, it is necessary to understand that rhythm, melody and harmony may move at different speeds. It is possible to conceive of infinite variations of rhythm without any change of harmony, but it is inconceivable for the harmony to move without affecting a change both in the melody and the rhythm. This trinity of rhythm, melody and harmony highlights the necessity for an individual point of view, not unlike a film director positioning the camera so that it has a point that views the situation as he sees fit. Nietzsche said they "there are no truths, but only interpretations," but music does not need interpretation. It needs observation of the written musical notation, control of its physical realization and a musician's capacity to become one with the work of another.

Nothing exists outside time: there is an indivisible connection in music, as well as in life, between tempo and substance. The speed of a harmonic progression, just like the speed of a political process, can determine its effectiveness and ultimately alter the reality it seeks to influence. I am convinced that the Israel-Palestine Oslo peace process, for example, was fated to fail—regardless of whether it was right or wrong—precisely because the relationship between content and time was erroneous. The preparation for the Oslo discussions took place much too hastily. The process itself, once the discussions began, was very slow and frequently interrupted, which gave it little chance of success. The equivalent in music would be to play a slow introduction much too quickly and haphazardly, and then to perform the main fast movement much too slowly and with interruptions. In both politics and music, speed and timing are not external factors but ones that irrevocably change the shape of things to come.

In music, everything must be constantly and permanently interconnected; the act of making music is a process of the integration of all its inherent elements. Unless the correct relationship between speed and volume is established, such integration is not complete and therefore cannot be called music in the fullest sense of the term. All elements in music must relate to each other. There are, of course, stylistic differences between composers: some means of expression, such as flexibility of volume and tempo, are possible in Puccini but wrong for Bach. The necessity of organically linking the various aspects of the music, though, is the same for all composers: Bach, Schoenberg, Puccini or Wagner.

A "feeling for music" can be defined as an instinctive or intuitive affect for sound as a means of expression. A feeling for music is insufficient, however, unless it is also combined with thought. It is impossible to be emotional without understanding in music, just as it is impossible to be rational without feeling— again, a very clear parallel with life. How do we live with discipline and passion? How do we make the connection between our brains and our hearts? In music we express emotion by broadening or accelerating the tempo, by changing the volume, the quality of the sound and the articulation, which means lengthening or shortening certain notes. If music can be defined as sound with thought, then none of these devices can be applied willfully; any technique must serve the higher purpose of expressing the music, and the performer must be the master who coordinates these elements, constantly connecting them, not allowing any element to remain independent of another.

Rational thought is also the guiding force that allows us to examine the attributes of courage and ambiguity in relation to music. A crescendo in Beethoven followed by a subito piano not only requires the ability to increase the volume and then abruptly reduce it. It also requires the ability to express the increase in volume in such a way that the ear anticipates a high point in the volume. Therefore unexpectedness is a necessary ingredient for the preparation of the subito piano. However *subito*, in Italian, means "sudden," a deviation from the expected. The increase in volume requires strategic, gradual preparation during the duration of the crescendo. The difficulty in executing this lies to a great degree in the interdependence of the extent of the increase and the control of its speed. If the sound increases disproportionately too soon, it will be impossible to carry the increase further at the later stages of the crescendo. If the sound does not increase enough, it will result either in insufficient increase at the later stages or a suddenness in the increase that will disrupt the quality of the crescendo. Therefore it is essential to know in advance the level of volume one wants to achieve at the height of the crescendo. It is essential, too, to know the level of volume of the subito piano. And it is necessary to be able to move decisively from the loudest point of the crescendo to the softest point of the subito piano. It is at this point that courage is required. The line of least resistance both musically and physically would dictate an adaptation consisting of an imperceptible lessening of the increase in order to facilitate the passage from the end of the crescendo to the subito piano. Courage, in this instance, means choosing the line of most resistance, by increasing the volume without taking into account the consequences of the abruptness of transition into the subito piano—not unlike walking confidently to the edge of a precipice and stopping at the very last possible moment. In relation to the production of sound, courage is defined by the willingness and ability to defy the expected. As Arnold Schoenberg said, "The middle way is the only way that does not lead to Rome." Each performer must find within himself the will required for this process, perhaps adopting the line of most resistance outside the world of sound as well.

Making music inevitably requires a point of view: not a willful, purely subjective point of view, but one based on total respect for the information received from the printed page, the understanding of the physical manifestations of sound and an understanding of the interdependence of all the elements in the music: harmony, melody, rhythm, volume and tempo. Total respect for the printed page means obeying what it says—playing piano, or soft where it says to and not capriciously changing it to forte. But how soft is piano? This simple question illustrates the importance of having a point of view regarding the quantity and the quality of the volume, in this case piano. Simply playing piano only because it says so on the printed page may be a sign of modesty, but it is also an instance of sinning by omission. The three permanent questions that a musician must ask himself are: why, how and for what purpose. The inability or unwillingness to ask these questions is symptomatic of a thoughtless faithfulness to the letter and an inevitable unfaithfulness to the spirit.

When Wagner begins the prelude of *Tristan und Isolde*, he starts the music out of nothing, on one note. If we listen carefully and intelligently, we can imagine that this note belongs to many tonalities, or musical keys. This creates a feeling of ambiguity and expectation that is absolutely essential in setting up the famous "*Tristan* chord" that arrives at the beginning of the second measure. If the previous measure had been fully written out and harmonically based, the dissonance of the *Tristan* chord would not have the same dramatic effect. But instead, Wagner first creates a situation of being in no-man's-land, harmonically and melodically. This is followed by a chord whose dissonance does not completely resolve, but is left suspended in mid-air. A composer with less genius and a poorer understanding of the mystery of music would assume that he must resolve the tension he has created. It is precisely the sensation caused by an only partial resolution, though, that allows Wagner to create more and more ambiguity and more and more tension as this process continues; each unresolved chord is a new beginning.

In life outside music, ambiguity is not necessarily a positive attribute—it is often a sign of indecision and, in politics, a lack of firm direction—but in the world of sound, ambiguity becomes a virtue in that if offers many different possibilities from which to proceed. Sound has the ability to make a link between all *elements*, so that no element is exclusively negative or positive. In music, even suffering can be pleasurable. Musicians, after all, also experience a feeling of pleasure when playing the funeral march of the Eroica Symphony. Feeling is an expression of the struggle for balance, and it cannot be allowed independence from thought. As Spinoza shows us, joy and its variants lead to a greater functional perfection; sorrow and its related affects are unhealthy and should therefore be avoided. In music, though, joy and sorrow exist simultaneously and therefore allow us to feel a sense of harmony. Music is always contrapuntal, involving an interplay of independent voices, in the philosophical sense of the word. Even when *it is linear*, there are always opposing elements coexisting, occasionally even in conflict with each other. Music accepts comments from one voice to the other at all times and tolerates subversive accompaniments as a necessary antipode to leading voices. Conflict, denial and commitment coexist at all times in music.

Music is not separated from the world; it can help us forget and understand ourselves simultaneously. In a spoken dialogue between two human beings, one waits until the other has finished what he has to say before replying or commenting on it. In music, two voices are in conversation simultaneously, each one expressing itself to the fullest, while at the same time listening to the other. We see from this the possibility of learning not only about music but from music—a lifelong process. Children can be taught order and discipline through rhythm. Young adults who experience passion for the first time and lose all sense of discipline can see through music how the two must coexist—even the most passionate phrase has to have an underlying sense of order. What is, ultimately, perhaps the most difficult lesson for the human being—learning to live with discipline yet with passion, with freedom yet with order—is evident in any single phrase of music.

We have already examined the indivisible connection in music between speed and substance, which is no different from the permanent interdependence between content and time: how time influences content by allowing events to develop in a certain way and how content in turn influences our subjective sense of time. Pleasure will render the passing of time subjectively faster; suffering or sadness will make it slower. Tempo rubato, literally "stolen time," is precisely the ability to give objective time a subjective quality. The slight modification required for tempo rubato gives both the musician and the listener the ability to ignore objective time, albeit for the duration of the tempo rubato. After all, it is the ear that determines audibility and transparency in music; it is the ear that must guide us in tempo rubato to have the moral strength to give back what was inadvertently stolen. The art of rubato lies in making imperceptible modifications of the tempo while maintaining a connection to it, an inner pulse. These modifications should be an exaggeration, but not an alteration, of certain elements in the rhythm. Furthermore, care should be taken that rubato is used only for a limited time, so as not to lose touch with the objective time that keeps ticking all along. As "stolen time", moreover, the tempo, morally speaking, demands to be returned at some point. The broadening of a certain passage or a certain group of notes must inevitably be followed by a passage or group of notes executed in a more flowing manner, so that the modification of tempo is only temporary, and the metronome running throughout the passage will be together with the music at the beginning and at the end, but not necessarily all the way through—much in the same way that a clock will show us the objective time regardless of our subjective perception. This may be the reason why Busoni said that music is simultaneously in time and outside time.

Modulation, the movement from one key to another, affects our perception of what we already know. In the Eroica Symphony, Beethoven introduces his main theme in the key of E flat, but in the recapitulation, when the theme reappears in the new key of F major, the new tonality gives the same music a different perspective. It is the same pattern seen from a different point of view. Modulation is also related to the concept of time: in order to achieve a different perspective in a foreign key, it is first necessary to spend a sufficient amount of time establishing the home key as such.

Because history, like music, moves in time, a single event can change not only how we approach the future but how we view the past. In music this occurs when a sudden vertical pressure is placed on the horizontal progression of the music, making it impossible for the music to continue as before. In the last movement of Beethoven's Ninth Symphony, the music comes to a complete stop on a sustained, fortissimo chord at the text, "*Und der Cherub steht vor Gott*" (and the cherub stands before God). The music modulates from A major to F major on the last repetition of the words "*vor Gott*," which are repeated independently of the rest of the sentence. What happens next could never have been predicted: when the music picks up again it is in a new key, a new tempo, a new meter and a new vein, leading the movement in an entirely different direction: just as, in a sense, the world was led in a different direction after November 1989, or September 11, 2001. Music teaches us that we have to accept the inevitability of an incident that changes the course of events irrevocably. Although one can have either an irrational sense of optimism or an irrational sense of pessimism following a great catastrophe, the ebb and flow of life, like the ebb and flow of music, are undeniable.

2

Listening and Hearing

Saint John said, "In the beginning there was the Word." Goethe said, "In the beginning there was the Deed." Perhaps one could also say, "In the beginning there was sound." Having already observed the relationship between sound and silence, I would now like to examine the relationship between the ear and the other organs of the body. It is a simple fact that sound is perceived by the ear. Aristotle said that the eyes are the organs of temptation and the ears the organs of instruction; not only does the ear take sound in, but by sending it directly to the brain it sets in motion an entire creative process of thought; the physical and cognitive processes of hearing are by no means passive.

The ear detects physical vibrations and converts them into signals, which then become sound sensations in the brain; the eye detects patterns of light and converts them into signals, which become visual images in the brain. The space occupied by the auditory system in the brain is smaller than the space occupied by the visual system. However, the neuroscientist Antonio Damasio says that the auditory system is physically much closer to those parts of the brain that regulate life, and which are the basis for the sense of pain, pleasure, motivation and other fundamental emotions. Furthermore, the physical vibrations that result in sound sensations are a variation on the sense of touch—they change the body directly and deeply, more so than the patterns of light that lead to vision. The human being has the capacity to close his eyes when he so desires. Furthermore, he needs outside help in order to see: light. He is, however, unable to close his ears. Sound penetrates the human body and is therefore more directly connected to it; in fact, sound is physical penetration over which the human being has no control.

The ear comes to life in the fetus of a pregnant woman on the forty-fifth day of pregnancy, which gives it a seven-and-a-half-month advance over the eye. But in our society, after the birth of the baby the ear is often neglected and the attention is focused almost exclusively on the eye. We live in a primarily visual society. Already in infancy the child is made more and more aware of what he sees, not of what he hears. When a small child is taught to cross the street, he is told to look both ways to make sure that no cars are coming, but not necessarily to listen for the sound of the vehicle approaching. In other words, we depend on the eye as a means of survival. Meanwhile, the neglect of the ear leads to the further impoverishment of our sense of hearing. In fact, it encourages us to hear without listening.

The importance of the ear cannot be overestimated. One of its functions is to help us remember and recollect, which means that it is not only an essential link to memory, but it forces us to do so with thought. Recollection, after all, is memory with thought; a young man remembers, an old man recollects. Memory is something that immediately comes to our aid, whereas recollection can only come through reflection and individual effort. The fact that the auditory system is physically close to the parts of the brain that regulate life accounts for the low's intelligence. According to Antonio Damasio, there are two fundamental types of memory: one related to skills, the other to facts. I would take this one step further and divide the fact-based memory into visual and auditory aspects. Each kind of memory requires the brain's participation in different degrees and ways.

Motoric memory, which is based on skill, is the brain's way of regulating the movements of the muscles and nerves. While playing a passage on the piano, for example, if all other types of memory have failed, often the fingers appear to remember automatically, circumventing a memory lapse. This implies an ability to detach the physical aspect of one's actions from rational thinking or effort, which would only get in the way at a time when doubt is already present. The motor control of the fingers, having learned a certain movement, or fingering, completes the sequence without the conscious participation of the intellect. On the other hand, visual memory, which is based on fact, requires greater conscious intellectual thought because it has fewer of the automatic qualities of motoric memory. Remembering a face inevitably means having noticed certain characteristics of the face, which then come to our aid when trying to remember it. A person looking at a painting controls the amount of time that he spends on each detail and this, of course, will affect his visual memory. The great pianist Arthur Rubinstein had an extraordinary visual memory. He once forgot his score of the Brahms D minor Piano Concerto in Paris when he came to perform it with me in New York, and the edition he was accustomed to was not available at the music store. He preferred not to buy a different edition of the piece because he was dependent on the visual memory of his own copy, knowing that on the third page there was a coffee stain. During the rehearsal he had an insignificant memory lapse and afterwards asked me to play for him, in private, the passage he had forgotten in the rehearsal, thus setting his auditory memory in motion to complement the visual memory.

Auditory memory can function on the basis of the subconscious—as it is possible to repeat mechanically a telephone number one has heard—but in other cases is connected to a rational reflection or observation that gives the brain the certainty of recollecting. The same telephone number will be more firmly installed in the memory if we create some pattern or order between the numbers that will help us remember. The creation of the pattern will deepen the encoding process of programming the memory. Music, of course, is much more complex than a telephone number, and a great deal of analysis and comprehension of the underlying structure is necessary in order to develop a solid memory of an entire piece. This is what I refer to as recollection: the completion of auditory memory by rational effort.

Repetition, for the ear, is a form of accumulation, thus becoming an essential ingredient in music itself. Music moves in time—therefore forward—but parallel and simultaneously to this progression, the ear remembers what it has already perceived—thereby moving backward, or even being conscious in the present and the past at once. We cannot have a memory of sound at the first note, but already by the second note we are aware of its relationship to the first note, because of the fact that the ear remembers the first note.

The comprehension of this physical dimension of sound leads to the metaphysical conclusion that no exact repetition is possible, because time has advanced and therefore places the second event in a different perspective. The ear creates the link between the present and the past, and sends signals to the brain as to what to expect of the future. In a musical sequence we remember the first statement, or musical subject, and the ear's memory leads us to expect to hear the same again. The structure of most Western music, regardless of its form, is bound to this principle.

The fugue is the form that approaches the principle of repetition in the most mathematical, direct and concise manner. In a three-voice fugue, for example, the main theme, or subject, is presented on its own, without accompaniment. Regardless of its length, it is in some ways unfinished because of the uncertainty of its development one cannot know how long it will be or how far it will stray from its starting point. This uncertainty is resolved only with the entrance of the second statement of the same subject. The subject can therefore only be perceived in its entirely once the second entrance of this subject has already begun. This is one of the many qualities that makes the fugue unique among musical forms: its statement is defined and framed by the arrival of its own repetition. The second entrance is a repetition of the same notes in another register and/or related key; the transposition of register or key has a similar effect to that of a sentence uttered by one person and immediately confirmed by a second, who speaks exactly the same words in a different voice. Meanwhile, the voice of the first subject becomes subsidiary to the second voice, thus creating a countersubject, and after the completion of the second statement both voices engage in a kind of transitional dialogue, which is known in musical terms as an episode. This is mostly unrelated to the main subject and is a transition required by the structure before the appearance of the third voice. This third voice proclaims the same truth in yet another register and then becomes the subject of geometric experimentation: it can be inverted, reversed, even stretched to twice its original length or reduced to half; in each case, however, the repetitions are easily recognizable to the trained ear. The ability to hear a fugue in all its complexity is akin to the ability to pick words out of a jumble of otherwise unrelated letters of the alphabet; the ear can be trained to remember and decipher all the different geometric versions of the subject, just as the eye, being trained to seek certain words, naturally finds them. In Bach's *Well-Tempered Clavier*, Fugue 6 in D minor, bars 1–14 demonstrate the first three entrances, episode and inverted subject in bar 14.

Sonata form is far less mathematical. If the fugue is epic, sonata form is dramatic. Whereas the fugue is highly contrapuntal and geometrical in the unfolding of its material, sonata form presents its subjects or themes in a more narrative fashion. Often, the first and second themes have opposing natures or characteristics: masculine/feminine, rhythmic/melodic and so on. The sense of drama in the work is created by the juxtaposition of these different characteristics. In fact, the introduction of the first theme in sonata form could be compared to the first entrance of a character in a play. At the beginning of the drama the character has no history within the context of the play. He may have a previous history that unfolds as the story is told, but with his initial appearance he has only a present and a future as far as the plot is concerned. Similarly, the entrance of the first theme sets the tone for the exposition in sonata form; everything that follows will be related to it. Once all the musical material is presented, the exposition reaches an end and the development section begins. The exposition is simply a presentation of the material in which all themes are allowed to tell their stories; each one is new to the world in which it exists. The development section, which follows the exposition, does exactly what it says. Even the most minute units of the given themes can be developed, and in the most unexpected ways; changes of tonality lead the musical material to venture into hitherto unexplored regions.

Changing the tonality of a theme alters the dramatic progression of a work in a way that can scarcely be explained in non-musical terms. Tonality, though, has a close relationship to spatial visualization. The distance between the two notes and the harmonic connection of one to the other are the basis for the expressive nature of an interval. The twelve notes of the Western musical scale have a distinct and clearly defined relationship to one another. These relationships have changed from one era to the next, sometimes from one composer to the next and sometimes between two works by the same composer, but certain inviolable rules have always governed the relationships between the notes of the scale. Certain changes of harmony, or modulations, are practically prescribed. In sonata form, for example, the first theme, which reappears at the beginning of the development section, will often do so in the dominant key, one fifth above the tonic, its original tonality. Even if the theme remains unchanged, its transposition into the key of the dominant literally transforms its position. The key of the dominant is the most obvious moment of harmonic tension that resolves into the tonic, thus creating the ebb and flow of tension and release. Having reached the dominant, it becomes far easier to enter new realms that are less closely related and less obvious consequences of the tonic key. The first modulation to the dominant key, then, opens the door to nearly endless possibilities of further modulation and exploration. This all takes place in a much less rigorous form than in the fugue, where the relationship of all episodes to the main subject is permanently present because of that subject's constant reappearances. In the development section of sonata form the themes are subject to internal transformation or development, thus generating uncertainty in contrast to the self-evident nature of their first entrances. The end of the development section prepares for the reappearance of material already known from the exposition. This third section, the recapitulation, is so called because it recapitulates the material from the exposition, which is now viewed from a different perspective because of what has transpired in the development section. The first theme, which in its initial appearance had only a present and a future, is now in the recapitulation the result of its own past: the exposition and the development section. At this point, if nothing else, the first theme is in an entirely different psychological situation. By the time the recapitulation is reached, the themes have undergone transformations; they are now recollecting or reliving something already known to them, but changed by the added knowledge and experience gained during the course of the movement. In this sense sonata form is not an epic narrative but rather a dramatic juxtaposition.[1]

Variation—to cite a third example of form in music—refers not only to an ornamental change but also to a process of transformation, which is in many cases a more correct word. Beethoven wrote many sets of variations, but in his magnum opus in variation form, the *Diabelli Variations* Op. 120, the original German title is *Dreiund dreissig Veränderungen*, which means "transformations." When a theme is transformed, it is subject to all the possible changes inherent in its own being. The word "variation" refers more to an observation of the nature of a theme's being and a comment on it, whereas transformation requires an understanding of the true essence of the object, changing its form without altering its nature. The transformation in Beethoven's masterwork applies to the rhythm, the dynamic, the pulse and, in fact, the meter: the theme of the *Diabelli Variations* is in 3/4 time like all waltzes, but already in the first variation the meter changes to 4/4. The notes of the melody remain the same but appear in completely different rhythmic, melodic and metric manifestations. It is a mathematical principle that the 3/4 meter can have only one main pulse—three can only be divided by one or three, and the inevitable progression of beats always leads us back to the one—but since four can be divided into two units there can be two main pulses in 4/4 time.[2]

In his great work, the Variations for Orchestra Op. 31, Schoenberg takes the process of transformation even further. He changes the meter, the harmony, and the rhythm, as Beethoven had done before him, but, of course, he has at his disposal an orchestra rather than a piano. This gives him the possibility further to transform the theme through changes of orchestration as well as a greater degree of flexibility in changing the register than is possible on the piano. In fact, these two great sets of variations make clear the connection between Beethoven and Schoenberg: both were able to summarize the music of their predecessors while at the same time showing the path to the future. Beethoven would have been impossible without Bach, Haydn and Mozart before him; equally, he paved the way for Schubert, Weber, Schumann, Brahms, ultimately arriving at Wagner. Schoenberg was able to make the seemingly opposing worlds of Brahms and Wagner coexist. He developed in his own music, for instance, Brahms's juxtaposition of the meters 3/2 and 6/4—in other words, the two mathematically possible divisions of six into either 3 × 2 or 2 × 3 (as in the third movement of the second piano concerto)—and simultaneously further developed Wagner's harmonic language. In *Tristan und Isolde*, Wagner stretched chromaticism to the point at which the tonality of the music became obscure, even cryptic. Schoenberg took it even further, beyond the point of no return, thus arriving at the twelve-tone system. The tonality of the prelude to *Tristan und Isolde* is so ambiguous that it only becomes clear in the concert ending of the prelude alone (written after the opera was completed and very rarely performed), in which it is concluded in A major. Schoenberg continued in this vein in his early works such as *Transfigured Night* or *Pelléas and Mélisande*, before totally obliterating the existence of harmony, giving each note in the twelve-tone scale equal importance. This was a radical break with the hierarchy that exists naturally in all tonal music. However, the human ear often seeks natural harmonic connections even when they are non-existent or irrelevant, which could lead us to believe that tonality is a law of nature and not of human invention. The paradox of the relationship between tonality and the twelve-tone system—the so-called abolition of tonality—is an example of the contradictions within human nature: one part of the psyche strives for freedom and independence regardless of the consequences, as evidenced in the constant struggle to break from tonality, while the other continues to seek the safety of hierarchy, authority and the familiar, demonstrated by the desire to seek, after all, the order of tonality.

Wagner understood the phenomenology of sound and the importance of the ear so well that he designed a theatre, the Festspielhaus in Bayreuth, where the orchestra is "sunk so deep that the spectator would look over it." He did not devise this, as people often claim, only so that the singers could be heard over the exceptionally large orchestra that he used. Rather, he needed to render the orchestra invisible and condemned "the constant visibility of the mechanism for tone production as an aggressive nuisance."[3] In other words, he also wanted to separate the ear from the eye, not allowing the eye to defect when the music was about to begin, since neither orchestra nor conductor can be seen. The magic of the Bayreuth Festspielhaus is most evident when the opera starts softly, as in *Das Rheingold, Tristan und Isolde*, or *Parsifal*, because there is no way of knowing when the sound is going to start, nor where it is coming from. Therefore the ear is doubly alert: the eye has to wait until the curtain goes up, whereas the ear has already perceived the nature of the drama.

This, of course, is linked to Wagner's conception of opera. Opera overtures before Wagner were very often brilliant pieces that were meant to attract the public's attention and prepare it for the work that was about to begin. The overture to *The Marriage of Figaro* actually has nothing to do with the opera that follows— one could almost play the overture to *Così fan Tutte* instead. Wagner, who was highly systematic in his thinking, believed that the overture should not only put the listener in the proper mood but also already involve him in a premonition of what is to come in the drama. As a result, the audience attaches itself to the first note and is unable to disengage itself from the world of sound, and consequently from the very essence of the drama from the start. This is why, in most cases, I think it is absolutely wrong to open the curtain earlier than Wagner indicates in the score and then to choreograph the music with imaginary action. Many stage directors raise the curtain at the very beginning of the music, because they want to fight against the separation of ear and eye, whereas this separation is actually an essential part of the process: first the understanding through the ear and only then the perception through the eye.

Listening to music is different from reading. When reading a book one reads the text and creates one's own associations, having only the text and one's own being to take into consideration. In listening to music there are physical laws of sound, time and space that have to be taken into account with every note. While listening to a piece of music at a concert it is impossible to repeat—to reread, as it were—a phrase or section that has not

been fully understood. The listener must alter his concentration—
his consciousness, even—in order to receive the musical material
while it is being performed. In order to immerse oneself fully in
the narrative of a book, one must create one's own experience of
the progression of time, or of the illusion of time passing through
the narrative; in music, however, this quality is a given. It is, of
course, possible to hear and not listen, as it is possible to look and
not see. Reading a book entails not only looking at the words but
also seeing them, converting the printed words into mental
constructs in order to understand the narrative. Likewise, listening to music entails hearing it as well, in order to understand the
musical narrative. Listening, therefore, is hearing with thought,
much in the same way as feeling is emotion with thought. When
an emotion arises it is not yet necessarily connected to any specific
event or person; it is the participation of the intellect that binds the
emotion to a particular set of circumstances, generating feeling.
The same process takes place when listening to a piece of music.

Recorded sound, which artificially preserves the unpreserva-
ble, increases the likelihood of listening without hearing, since it
can be listened to at home or in motion, thus allowing us
to reduce music to background activity and eliminate the
possibility of total concentration—i.e., thought. The moral
responsibility for this rests entirely with the individual human
being, who can determine whether a recording is a means of
instruction, rendering the music more familiar through repetition—the equivalent of rereading a passage in a book—or
simply a means of distraction in the sense of the music played by
the band in Thomas Mann's *The Magic Mountain*, to which the
philosopher Settembrini says,

> The human being, unfortunately, has a tendency to imbue objects
> with moral authority, so as not to take the responsibility himself.
> Is a knife an instrument with which one can commit murder—
> therefore an immoral instrument—or is it an instrument with

which bread can be cut and a fellow human being fed—therefore an instrument of human generosity? It is the human being's application of it that determines its moral qualities.

Under close observation, the power of the ear becomes noticeable even when music is intentionally designed as background accompaniment, as in film. The famous shower scene in Alfred Hitchcock's *Psycho* is driven by the music. We need only imagine it with another type of music—maybe the New Year's Day concert of the Vienna Philharmonic—to realize that it could be far from frightening, even though the eye is telling us what to expect. In fact, Hitchcock had not planned to have music accompany the murder scene until he realized how much more powerful it was with the soundtrack Bernard Herrmann had written. In this case, when the eye and the ear work together, we see that the ear is stronger than the eye. (Bravo, Richard Wagner!)

We have become increasingly insensitive to information that we receive through the ear. The lack of sensitivity that is evident so often in uncontrolled coughing in concert halls leads to far worse manifestations. The visual equivalent of these offenses— the most despicable aspects of pornography, for example—are perceived as so terrible that the people who commit them are accused of disturbing society. Yet many atrocities, which are just as upsetting to the ear, are routinely ignored. Not only do we neglect the ear but we often suppress the signals it sends to our brains as well. More and more in our society (not only in the United States, although the Americans were certainly active in starting this process) we create opportunities to hear music without listening to it—with what is commonly known as Muzak. Is it reasonable to expect somebody to listen to the Brahms Violin Concerto in the elevator and then to have to play or listen to it in the concert hall? This misuse of music will not convert a single person into an advocate of classical music. It is not only counterproductive but, seen in terms of musical ethics, it is absolutely offensive. Muzak cannot possibly provide a full experience of music because music requires silence and total concentration on the part of the listener. Muzak is, in fact, intended to create exactly the kind of indifferent satisfaction described by Settembrini in *The Magic Mountain*, replacing the participation of the intellect with passive consumption.

Today, particularly in the United States, there is a fixation on descriptive marketing, which often not only forcefully reduces music to background noise, but also creates false associations. Beethoven's Fifth Symphony was certainly not meant to make us think of chocolates, as one American chocolate manufacturer would like us to believe. As a result of the images imposed on pure music, the public is made to forget the necessity to listen and concentrate. It is therefore natural to think that it is sufficient to be present at the musical performance without actively listening to it. The listener may even expect associations to awaken within himself that are in fact unrelated to the music and inevitably render him unable to have a musical experience.

One day, while watching television in Chicago, I came across the most extraordinary example of the offensive usage of music in a commercial for a company called American Standard. In this commercial, a plumber was shown running very fast in great agitation, opening the door to a lavatory and demonstrating the superiority of a particular toilet. The whole visual sequence was accompanied by the Lacrimosa from Mozart's *Requiem*. Some viewers were understandably offended by the use of Mozart's music as an aural backdrop for the sale of toilets, and they wrote letters to various newspapers and to the company itself. They received the following reply:

> Thank you for contacting American Standard with your concerns about the background music in the current television commercial

for our champion toilet. We appreciate that you have taken the time to communicate with us, and share your feelings on a matter that clearly is very important to you. When we first selected Mozart's *Requiem*, we didn't know of its religious significance. We actually learned about it from a small number of customers like you, who also contacted us. Although there is ample precedent for commercial use of spiritual theme music, we have decided to change it to a passage from Wagner's *Tannhäuser* Overture, which music experts have assured us does not have religious importance. The new music will begin airing in June.

It is obvious that American Standard could not conceive of any reason for the viewers' outrage other than blasphemy. The idea that the true blasphemy might consist of the abuse of a musical work of art may never have occurred to the company's customer relations representative, who chose to attribute the offense to the customers' religious, non-musical associations.

Although unintentional, the use of Mozart's music in television advertising creates a widespread familiarity with a minuscule excerpt of his *Requiem*, taken out of context and subject to non-musical associations: in this case, the need to buy a new toilet. This kind of familiarity is anything but beneficial to the state of classical music today. Using fragments of great works of music to infiltrate popular culture (or the lack thereof) is not the solution to the crisis in classical music. Accessibility does not come through populism; accessibility comes through greater interest, curiosity and knowledge. Certain locations are described as being "wheelchair-accessible." To make a building "wheelchair-accessible", one simply needs to place ramps or lifts wherever there are stairs. In the case of classical music, education is the ramp, or the lift, that makes it accessible. Concentration on music is an activity that must begin at a very early age in order for it to develop organically, like the understanding of spoken language. It then becomes a necessity rather than a luxury. The mastery of a musical instrument, however, is not a prerequisite for the ability to understand or concentrate on a piece of music; listening to music need not be a passive activity.

In his treatise *Politics*, Aristotle writes that "no one will doubt that the legislator should direct his attention above all to the education of youth; for the neglect of education does harm to the constitution. The citizen should be molded to suit the form of government under which he lives. For each government has a peculiar character which originally formed and which continues to preserve it. The character of democracy creates democracy, and the character of oligarchy creates oligarchy; and always the better the character, the better the government." There is a tremendous amount to be learned for life through music, and yet our current system of education neglects this realm entirely, from kindergarten right through to the last years of school. Even in music schools and conservatories, the instruction is highly specialized and often unrelated to the actual content, and thus the power, of music. The availability of recordings and films of concerts and operas stands in inverse proportion to the poorness of musical knowledge and understanding prevalent in our society. The current state of public education is responsible for a population that is able to listen to almost any piece of music at will, but unable to concentrate on it fully.

The education of the ear is perhaps far more important than we can imagine not only for the development of each individual but for the functioning of society, and therefore also of governments. Musical talent and understanding, and auditory intelligence, are areas that are so often separated from the rest of human life, relegated either to the function of entertainment or to the esoteric realm of elite art. The ability to hear several voices at once, comprehending the statement of each separate one; the capacity to recollect a theme that made its first entrance before a long process of transformation and now reappears in a different light; and the aural skill of recognizing the geometrical variations of a fugue subject are all qualities that enhance understanding. Perhaps the cumulative effect of these skills and abilities could form human beings more apt to listen to and understand several points of view at once, more able to judge their own place in society and in history, and more likely to apprehend the similarities between all people rather than the differences between them.

3

Freedom of Thought and Interpretation

I read Spinoza's *Ethics* for the first time when I was thirteen years old. Of course at school we studied the Bible—which for me is the ultimate philosophical work. However, reading Spinoza opened up a new dimension for me, which is the reason for my continuing dedication to his works. Spinoza's simple principle "man thinks" has become an existential mind-set for me; my copy of his *Ethics* has become dog-eared and torn. For years I took it with me on my travels, and in hotel rooms or intervals in concerts became absorbed by many of its principles. Spinoza's *Ethics* is the best training ground for the intellect, above all because Spinoza teaches the radical freedom of thought more completely than any other philosopher.

This Spinozan brand of freedom is not a release from discipline into arbitrariness of thought, but an active process. The more one is able to determine one's own thoughts—in fact, causing one's own thoughts, thereby creating one's own experience of reality— the more it is possible to become self-determined and to be truly free. It is quite easy to believe oneself free in modern Western civilization, having so many choices—the choice of where to live, what to read, what to watch on television or on the Internet— when in fact this kind of freedom requires a keen awareness of one's appetites. Without this, one is simply the slave of these appetites and not in possession of the power to shape one's own ideas and actions.

This awareness has become a kind of pre-Freudian self-analysis for me; Spinoza helps me to see myself and my surroundings objectively. This can make life bearable even throughout the experience of suffering; the teachings presented in the *Ethics* allow one to perceive the world as a manageable place. Freud himself once wrote in a letter to Bickel, "I admit my dependence on Spinoza's teachings." Conversely, Spinoza admits, foreshadowing Freudian analysis, that we cannot be in complete control over our emotions. In the *Ethics* (proposition 7, part 4) he writes: "An emotion can neither be restrained nor removed except by an emotion which is contrary to and stronger than the one which is to be restrained." It is not sufficient, for example, to understand intellectually that jealousy has a negative effect on the organism; it must be countered by an equally strong emotion—generosity, perhaps, or love. The ability to create emotional balance, though, is dependent upon the intellectual awareness of the problem. In this way Spinoza demands the integration of all human aspects in order to attain true freedom.

In music, too, intellect and emotion go hand in hand, both for the composer and for the performer. Rational and emotional perception are not only not in conflict with one another; rather, each guides the other in order to achieve an equilibrium of understanding in which the intellect determines the validity of the intuitive reaction, and the emotional element provides the rational with a dimension of feeling that renders the whole human. Some musicians fall prey to the superstitious belief that too thorough an analysis of a piece of music will destroy the intuitive quality and freedom of their performance, mistaking knowledge for rigidity and forgetting that rational understanding is not only possible but absolutely necessary in order for the imagination to have free reign.

The great Voltaire once accused Spinoza of "abusing metaphysics." Today, though, the uncompromising nature of metaphysics has become more important than ever. To think in a metaphysical way means, etymologically, to go beyond the physical, the tangible and the literal in order to comprehend both the essence of a thing and its relationship to all other things, be it a person, a government, a voice in a Bach fugue or an event in history. Liberated thinking has, in fact, become one of our most valuable freedoms in an era in which political systems, social constraints, moral codes and political correctness often control our thinking.

Another inevitable constraint on free thought is the attempt to facilitate the condition of human existence by constructing a system of belief that renders the act of questioning futile. Without a doubt, there is great effort inherent in the formulation of questions regarding one's existence, an effort circumscribed by fears of being unable to answer such questions or, worse yet, of finding disconcerting answers. But this effort is the most powerful weapon available against dogma; the very idea of search requires the will and courage to learn in stages without any guarantee of acquiring knowledge at the end of the process. The search for a system of belief, on the other hand, is the beginning of the basis of ideology and fundamentalism. An idea that is swallowed by a system is stripped of its essence and of the energy with which it was conceived. A system is by nature a set of rules for the application of ideas and principles that preclude the necessity of further thought, whereas an idea is by nature in a constant process of development. One could say that an idea has the potential to transcend fixed concepts, obtaining a metaphysical perspective, whereas a system remains earthbound and inflexible in its point of view.

Ideology in any form or manifestation is not the expression of an idea; it is merely a vehicle for its implementation. No idea can be implemented in all of its aspects at one time, just as a performer can present only certain aspects of the music in one performance, but cannot express everything contained within the score. The distilled essence of an idea, which is infinite, must not be confused with its implementation, which is finite. The essence of an idea is not subject to change over time, whereas its implementation is variable, depending on time, perception and understanding. The ability to distinguish between idea and ideology and to choose to re-examine one's principles rather than to be satisfied with a pre-packaged solution is not simply a challenge to the intellect but also to the character. In other words, a human being who has an idea and has observed the way this idea has functioned in the past wants to believe that it can be applied to other situations without any further search. This is an example of what Spinoza calls empirical knowledge, acquired merely through the observation of recurring patterns or habits and not from an understanding of the essence. This empirical knowledge is, in philosophical terms, mutilated and confused or simply incomplete. Having observed that the sun appears and disappears every day, it is possible to claim to know that the sun will continue to appear and disappear every day; however, this is according to Spinoza knowledge of a very low grade since it does not include the understanding and ability to explain *why* this is so.

Spinoza also speaks of two other, higher kinds of knowledge, the second being reason and consisting of "common notions and adequate ideas of the properties of things" (second scholium, proposition 40 of part 2 of the *Ethics*). This is the knowledge not of a particular manifestation of something, such as a specific circle, but of circles in general. The third kind of knowledge, intuitive knowledge, enables one to know about a particular thing without the necessity of demonstration, as this would belong to the second kind of knowledge.* This category of intuitive knowledge has

---

* To take a mathematical example, in order to find a fourth proportional (given three numbers, finding a fourth which is to the third what the second is to the first, for example 1, 2, 3, 6) one must multiply the second number by the third and divide the product by the first. For somebody who knows only by experience (first kind of knowledge), this has always worked with small numbers and must therefore work with all numbers. One who uses reason (second kind of knowledge) will relate this rule to mathematical proof, in this case Euclid. But with intuitive knowledge (third kind of knowledge) the rule is not necessary because we *see* the fourth number without an operation. We think of the rule in the particular instance, but we do not calculate.

been criticized by many for being somewhat obscure and incomprehensible, but it is this knowledge that Spinoza deemed to be the most powerful.

Even the most intelligent and humane ideas need constantly to be subjected to further scrutiny, if nothing else because of the relationship between content and time; our understanding of ideas is in permanent transformation in the progression of linear time. The principles of the French Revolution, for instance—liberty, equality, fraternity—cannot simply be engraved in stone, but must be re-evaluated and adapted to new realities. Bach's music, too, can be expressed in the stylistic language of more than one age but must be approached anew with each performance.

The great advances in technology and communications media in our time have, in many ways, led to a general tendency to be satisfied with slogans, which are not just poor substitutes but aberrations of the ideas they claim to represent. This shorthand version of knowledge, when accepted at face value, can lead to mental laziness. Information is presented on television and on the Internet in a way that does not allow enough time for reflection and comprehension, thus turning powerful and potentially very positive inventions into the ideal tools for the manipulation of the general public. I sometimes wonder whether a Hitler or a Goebbels would have been able to achieve such popularity without the help of radio and newsreels. Thanks to the development of new technology, it is easier and faster than ever before to find information about almost anything, but this information is accepted in a passive way for the most part, and there is no room for educated discussion among all these superfluous facts, even on the Internet. Discussion requires thought—the formulation of ideas—and an idea needs time to be developed and to express itself.

To allow an idea to grow and remain flexible requires not only constant intellectual exploration but also the ability to re-examine one's own position in an objective light. With experience and through repetition, we tend to yield to the validity of empirical knowledge, taking the path of least resistance. In contrast, to paraphrase Spinoza, a strong character strives for the transformation of observation into understanding—from empirical knowledge to an understanding of the essence—which requires the second and third kinds of knowledge. This higher knowledge prevents the influence of false prejudices, allowing one to lead a life of reason, which for Spinoza is synonymous with freedom. Reason should pervade all thought, emotion and human activity, according to Spinoza.*

The leitmotif of the *Ethics* of Spinoza is that we base our finitude in the infinite. Man is a finite being, since he is not absolutely self-determined—in other words, not the cause of himself. Only God is the cause of Himself (*causa sui*), and in this capacity He is also the cause of all things, including man. Therefore man's finitude is based on the infinite; when one acquires true knowledge—knowledge of the second and third kinds—and is active in Spinoza's sense of intellectual and emotional creation, one increases one's power and approaches the infinite.

In the same way, the finitude of any musical interpretation is based on the infinity of possibilities at our disposal. The score is the final substance, the finished work, and the interpretation of it

---

* He writes: "All the prejudices that I undertake to point out here depend on one fact: that men commonly suppose that all natural things act on account of an end, as they themselves do." It is ignorance that causes these prejudices to be so strong, the ignorance of how things function in reality. When man out of ignorance starts to believe, for example, that God created the world *for* man, he invents absurd constructions in order to make his conception of the world fit with reality. "From this it came about that each person, in accordance with his own way of thinking, thought out different ways of worshipping God, so that God might love them above the rest, and direct the whole of Nature to the advantage of their blind desire and insatiable avarice. So this prejudice turned into a superstition, and put down deep roots in the mind, which was the cause of the fact that each person endeavoured mightily to understand and to explain the final causes of all things. But whilst they tried to show that Nature does nothing in vain (that is, nothing that is not to the advantage of men), they seem to have shown simply that Nature and the gods are as mad as men."

is a finite, temporary expression that takes place in time and has a beginning and an end. To be able to grasp the substance of the music itself is to be willing to begin a never-ending search. The task of the performing musician, then, is not to express or interpret the music as such, but to aim to become part of it. It is almost as if the interpretation of the musical text creates for itself a subtext that develops, substantiates, varies and contrasts the actual text. This subtext is inherent in the score and is itself boundless; it results from a dialogue between the performer and the score, and its richness is determined by the curiosity of the performer. In the theater the function of such a subtext is more obvious: the stage director and actors or singers are obligated to tell the story while also exploring the subjective and objective conditions that influence each character. To be "faithful to the score," a phrase one hears so often, means so much more than its literal reproduction in sound; seen from this perspective, there is no such thing as absolute faithfulness to the score. Literacy is only half of the equation, the other half being made up of the questioning that leads us to search for and understand each part of the music in terms of the ultimate nature of the whole.

One of Spinoza's most important conclusions is that of the human being's necessity to overcome the contradiction between the finite and the infinite. Spinoza was able to express the very nature of the Judeo-Christian way of thought and, at the same time, to remain outside it and even negate it. Both in the Jewish and the Christian traditions, God creates the world but is outside it. Spinoza, on the other hand, would not say that God creates the world, but that He produces it—in philosophical terms, He causes it. God, for Spinoza, is not outside the world, and this view was the object of very harsh criticism by his contemporaries. The Jewish community in Holland even saw fit to excommunicate him. The God of Judeao-Christian thought, according to Spinoza, is an invention of man, who imagines that God thinks and acts as human beings do. Kierkegaard, as an example of purely Christian

philosophical thought, speaks of the recognition by the finite
creature—the human being—of his debt to the infinite creator,
whereas Spinoza believed in the need to overcome the contradiction between the finite and the infinite.

This not only provides the key to the interpretation of music
but also to the understanding of human nature. As performers we
must accept the printed score as an infinite substance while not
forgetting that we are finite, temporary. As human beings we must
acknowledge that we are individually all equally finite in relation
to the infinite depth of human nature. Paradoxically, the essence
of our finitude is precisely our striving to exist for ever, to become
infinite. No human being, unless at the edge of despair, has the
free will to cease existing. Very often we imagine changing the
course of our lives according to interest or need, and it is a
fascinating but very difficult exercise to imagine the directions we
could have taken at different points in our lives.

However, such an exercise is not essentially relevant to our
lives. In music, however, it is helpful to imagine what a composer
would have written had he chosen to go in a different direction, be
it in a melodic, harmonic or rhythmic sense. The opening to the
prelude of *Tristan und Isolde* would be entirely different if the first
statement in the opening three bars had a full harmonic resolution
before proceeding to a repetition of this statement. As it is written,
it leads only to a partial harmonic resolution. In the same way it is
interesting to imagine how the world would be different today if,
for example, more than one superpower existed and the Cold War
continued to prevail. The unilateralism of American policies
today is not only a result of the American way of thinking
but, even more so, the result of the fact that there is no power in
the world today capable of counterbalancing the United States.

A nation's constitution could be compared to a score and the
politicians its interpreters, who must constantly act and react
according to the principles outlined within it. In a democracy this
constitution can be challenged and adapted to changing times by

the people, becoming a kind of collectively composed symphony. Just as a performer must be constantly vigilant and curious enough to re-examine formerly conceived notions of interpretation and performance, a politician must be aware of his nation's actions as well as its lack of action in regard to the principles by which his constituents have chosen to live. Spontaneity is required both of the performer and of the politician, who must be flexible enough to adjust their ideas of what must be done to the current reality. Here it is worth pointing out that there is a significant difference between spontaneity, or flexibility, and a lack of conception, or strategic thought. Flexibility is imperative for the survival of democracy, which thrives on a constant dialogue between voters, politicians and policies.

Democracy is an idea that originated in Greece thousands of years ago. Over the centuries and millennia the original idea has been lost, as exemplified by contemporary manifestations of the democratic process. In ancient Greece, only the sages of society could vote and determine the government's course of action for the public good. Today we have made the right to vote ubiquitous, and very rightly so, but have denied the voters the opportunity of a complete education. The political world of today is modern only in its outward manifestations; technology has made communication far more efficient, which unfortunately has led to an exploitation and manipulation of the uneducated population. The average voter in our society is not well versed in any of the arts or sciences—which were, according to ancient Greek thought, so essential to any understanding of government—and is unable to think beyond the present and the immediate future to understand fully the consequences of political action. The result is a doubly poor society in which politicians are forced to act tactically rather than strategically in order to remain in power long enough to make any changes and the public is manipulated while remaining ignorant about the most vital issues.

One of the most important aspects of political thinking is the ability to use strategy in order to change the state of things, not unlike a composer who strategically constructs his composition, first presenting the material and only later transforming it. A performer, too, must be able to hear the last note of a piece in his inner ear before playing the first; in order to do this, he must create his own physical "realization" of the score—a term I prefer to the much-abused word "interpretation"—in a strategic rather than a tactical way, acting rather than reacting. The tactical approach is constantly subject to the performer's reaction to harmonic, rhythmic and melodic elements as they occur, and cannot result in the construction of an organic whole made up of all of these elements. Only a strategically thinking performer is able to communicate the structure of a piece of music to the listener, and not simply the different moods that occur within the piece.

Becoming truly free and spontaneous as a performer is akin to becoming the master of one's own thoughts according to Spinoza's principles. Just as it is easy to confuse the right to think freely with freedom of thought, it is also possible to feel spontaneous in performance while in fact being limited by the tendency to react to musical events as they occur. Legend has it that the eighth-century Arab poet Abu Nuwas once visited the renowned Khalaf Al Ahmar to seek his advice on how to write poetry and was told to begin by memorizing one thousand poems. After having accomplished the task, he recited them from memory to the master, who now instructed him promptly to forget them. This fable, oversimplified though it is, describes exactly the process that a musician must undergo when studying an un-familiar work. In other words the structure of a work must become so internalized in the mind of the musician that intellec-tual thought during the performance is no longer necessary; on the other hand he may trust that his spontaneous promptings arise from his deep knowledge of the work and not from personal whim.

When I read or play a score for the first time, there is no objective possibility of having either familiarity or an intellectual understanding of the piece; the initial reaction is exclusively instinctive, the result of a first impression. The most talented musician in the world will not be able to analyze at first sight. After this initial contact, I can proceed to an analysis of the piece, work on it, think about it, turn it upside down, and in so doing acquire far more knowledge of the music than I had upon the original reading of it. Generally, at this stage of the proceedings, a lot of the freshness of the first contact may have been lost. The first intuitive reaction was the beginning of a process, which has now become primarily rational, and my main concern is to understand the anatomy of the piece, which is a condition for the ability to express its structure. I need to observe the relationships between all the different elements of the music. Having the structure in mind, though, is only part of the necessary path to a real understanding of the music. The next step is the result of knowing the material in the most detailed way, which allows me to relive the first encounter, but this time with a kind of conscious naïveté, which allows me to unfold the piece as if the music is being composed as I play it. Very often, after having worked in depth this way, something will unexpectedly occur to me during the performance, making me go in a direction that never struck me in all the times that I had played it in private. This spontaneous realization, though, would not have been possible without all the repetitions and the familiarity resulting from intense study. This is why improvisation—going in an unexpected direction, allowing the fingers, the heart, the brain, the gut, to cooperate in an unpremeditated way—is a very blessed state in the life of a human being, as well as the basis for making music.

There is no substitute for knowledge, self-knowledge, or a metaphysical understanding of the score and one's relationship to it; and no amount of talent or even training can compensate for the lack of all these elements. "Man thinks," says Spinoza, and this thinking is the result of a dialogue between the intellect, the emotions and the intuition. This is not only true of the thinking of each individual, but of groups of people and even of nations. As we have seen in the history of the Middle East, the exclusion of one or more parties from dialogue can have disastrous consequences, even resulting in terrorism. The inclusion of all parties in a dialogue, whether in international politics or in an individual's consciousness, is not a guarantee for perfect harmony, but it creates the conditions necessary for cooperation.

4

The Orchestra

Edward Said said that music is a little bit subversive. Like so many things in music, this says more about how we perceive it than about the music itself. He was unquestionably right, though: in music, different notes and voices meet and are linked to each other, either in joint expression or in counterpoint, which means exactly that—one point, or note, working against another. But in the act of challenging each other, the two voices fit together perfectly, even complementing one another. There is a permanent aural hierarchy in all music that consists of main, subsidiary and accompanying voices. The relationship between the main and subsidiary voices is clearly defined by their respective functions. The relationship between these voices and their accompaniment, however, is less obvious; the accompaniment can support or complement the main or subsidiary voices, but it can also act in a subversive way, characterizing the music in such a way that it forces the main voices to be permanently aware of the accompanying figure. Important as it is, this accompaniment must never allow itself to question the prominence of the main voices. In chamber music and in the orchestra, one of the greatest challenges to the balance of the ensemble is that instruments, or groups of instruments, that play long passages of accompaniment have a tendency to forget their own importance and resort to passive execution of the notes. It must for example be very disconcerting to play the second violin or viola part in a Rossini overture, where the main subject is in the first violins or the winds, especially if one feels one has something else to contribute. The paradox of such frustration, though, is that a musician who loses his objective awareness of the relationship between his voice and the main voice not only sabotages the prominence of the main voice but also detracts from his own contribution. The Austrian conductor Josef Krips put it rather succinctly, if not in very professional musical terminology, when he said that accompaniments in Mozart must be aristocratic or plebeian, but never bureaucratic.

The slow movement of Beethoven's Pathétique sonata opens with a relatively simple melody. When we examine it closely, we see that there is a main voice that weaves its way through the whole passage and a subsidiary bass line that accompanies it, in the most complete sense of the word—not merely following, but having its own say, going up when the melody goes down and vice versa—thereby conversing with and influencing each other. At the same time there is a middle voice present that provides a sense of continuity and fluidity.[1]

In the last prelude from Book One of Bach's *Well-Tempered Clavier*, three different voices each vie for our attention at different times. The two upper ones are equally important and secure in their primacy, allowing themselves a dialogue between equals. The bass line has a slow continuous movement, which has a much less important melodic function, but which is able to influence the dialogue of the two upper voices by way of harmonic changes, which force the main voices to be constantly vigilant.[2]

Even in the operatic arias of Bellini, Donizetti, or Verdi, in which it is clear that there is only one main voice singing on the stage and the orchestra merely provides the accompaniment, it is evident that the accompaniment performs an important rhythmic and harmonic function, influencing and characterizing the singing line in a very obvious way.

Schoenberg went so far as to make clear distinctions in the importance of different voices by marking the principal line

Hauptstimme (leading voice) and marking the secondary part *Nebenstimme* (subsidiary voice, or commentary). The hierarchy that exists in all music respects the individuality of each voice, which may not have the same rights but certainly has equal responsibility as all the other voices. This, of course, is much easier to achieve in music than in life; how difficult it is in the world to create equality within hierarchy![3]

In times of totalitarian or autocratic rule, artists have often been able to remain true to themselves under otherwise very restricting circumstances. Culture, in this context, has frequently been the only avenue of independent thought. It is the only way people can meet as equals and exchange ideas freely; it becomes the primary voice of the oppressed and takes over from politics as a driving force for change. Often, in societies suffering from political oppression, or from a vacuum in leadership, culture takes a dynamic lead, changing external realities by influencing the collective consciousness of the people. There are many extra-ordinary examples of this phenomenon: Samizdat writings in the former Eastern Bloc; South African poetry and drama under apartheid; Palestinian literature in the midst of deep conflict. Conversely, totalitarian regimes have abused their native artists, presenting their works as the culmination of a highly efficient and richly cultured society—one of the most cynical exploitations imaginable, since it purposely alters the spirit of artistic creativity.

One of the most obvious victims of this kind of exploitation was the Russian composer Dmitri Shostakovich, who expressed through his music the oppressive nature of life in the Soviet Union. Stalin misused Shostakovich's international popularity by maintaining that his music represented a portrayal of positive Soviet values. This deliberate political misunderstanding went so far as to influence the performance of Shostakovich's music in the West, where it acquired a one-dimensional character and super-ficial brilliance very far removed from the sarcasm or irony intended by the composer.

Culture encourages contact between people and can bring them closer together, fostering understanding. This is why Edward Said and I founded the West-Eastern Divan project, as a way to bring together musicians from Israel, Palestine and the other Arab countries to make music together, and ultimately—when we realized how much interest there was for the idea—to form an orchestra. We took the name of our project, the West-Eastern Divan, from a collection of poems by Goethe, who was one of the first Europeans to be genuinely interested in other cultures. He originally discovered Islam when a German soldier who had been fighting in one of the Spanish campaigns brought back a page of the Koran to show to him. His enthusiasm was so great that he started to learn Arabic at the age of sixty. Later he discovered the great Persian poet Hafiz and that was the inspiration for his set of poems dealing with the idea of the other, *The West-Eastern Divan*, which was first published nearly two hundred years ago, in 1819. At the same time, interestingly enough, Beethoven was writing his Ninth Symphony, his celebrated testament to fraternity—to the brotherhood of mankind.

Goethe's poems became a symbol for the idea behind our experiment in bringing Arab and Israeli musicians together. This experiment began in 1999 in Weimar, which made it all the more appropriate to name the orchestra after Goethe's collection of poems. This small town in Thuringia represents in many ways both the best and the worst of German history: from the seventeenth to the nineteenth centuries it was the cultural home of Goethe, Schiller, Bach and Liszt, and the town is full of monuments and museums dedicated to these great figures and their intellectual achievements. Since the Second World War, though, the Buchenwald concentration camp, only a short distance away, has cast its shadow over even the highest, noblest intentions of humanity and has served as a constant reminder of the opposite extreme: the human potential for cruelty, inhumanity and devastation. This complex history, which has since become intertwined with the history of the state of Israel, set the stage for the first session of the orchestra, which consists of young people from Palestine and the occupied territories, Palestinians from Israel, Syrians, Lebanese, Jordanians, Egyptians and of course Israelis.

Whenever one plays music, whether it is chamber music or in an orchestra, one has to do two very important things simultaneously. One is to express oneself—otherwise one is not contributing to the musical experience—and the other is to listen to the other musicians, an imperative facet of music making. In the case of string players the other person may be one's neighbor, sharing a stand and playing the same part. As a wind player, the other may be playing a different instrument in counterpoint to one's own voice. In any case it is impossible to play intelligently in an orchestra while concentrating on only one of these two things. To play one's own part very well is not enough; without listening it may become so loud that it covers the other parts, or it may become so soft that it cannot be heard. On the other hand listening is also not enough. The art of playing music is the art of simultaneous playing and listening, one enhancing the other. This takes place both on an individual and a collective level: the playing is enhanced by the listening and one voice is enhanced by another. This dialogical quality inherent in music was our main reason for founding the orchestra. Edward Said made it clear in his discussions with the young musicians that separation between people is not a solution for any of the problems that divide us, and ignorance of the other certainly provides no help whatsoever.

Our intention in the workshop was to start a dialogue, to take a single step forward and to find common ground between estranged peoples. With excitement we witnessed what happened when an Arab musician shared a music stand with an Israeli musician, both trying to play the same note with the same dynamic, the same stroke of the bow, the same sound, the same expression. They were trying to do something together about which they were both passionate because, after all, indifference and music making cannot coexist. Music demands a permanently passionate attitude regardless of the level of aptitude. The fundamental principle of the orchestra was quite simple: once the young musicians agreed on how to play even just one note together they would not be able to look at each other in the same way again. If, in music, they were able to carry on a dialogue by playing simultaneously, then ordinary verbal dialogue in which one waits until the other has finished would become considerably easier. That was our starting point, and from the beginning Edward and I were filled with optimism despite what he termed the darkening sky, with what has sadly turned out to be all too accurate foresight.

I have come to believe that morality and strategy are not exclusive of one another, but rather go hand in hand in the Israel-Palestine conflict, in the same way that it is impossible to separate rational understanding from emotional involvement in music. The dialogue between intellect and emotion can also temper an unquestioning attitude to religion, forming an important voice in counterpoint to the potential monotony of religious fervor. The Old Testament, the New Testament and the Koran are all sources of infinite wisdom when read from an independent, questioning point of view; reading these texts philosophically gives us not only an understanding of history but also of human behavior. They cannot, however, provide the sole guidelines for human existence if they are interpreted literally or without the participation of all facets of human intelligence. Former German chancellor Helmut Schmidt supported this view with descriptions of several experiences from his long political career in a speech he made in Marburg, Germany, in February 2007. In many cases, he contended, it was impossible to make extremely difficult decisions without the aid of reason. Religious and moral beliefs had to be isolated from the matter at hand, whether it was the decision to prolong the statute of limitations on murder, or negotiations with terrorists who had kidnapped a member of the German government. In cases such as these there was no help to be sought from religious texts and no justification for relying on one's morality. Reason alone was responsible for carrying him through these trying situations.

With this notion we return to Spinoza's axiom that man thinks, and that without thought, he is inevitably reduced. Music and religion share a common preoccupation with the relationship between human beings, and between man and the universe. Involvement with music requires a permanent search for a whole in spite of the infinite diversity in any particular work; in religion this has its parallel in the individual's striving for oneness with the Creator. Religion, though, is primarily concerned with man's relationship to the universe, whereas Western classical music is more interested in exploring the depth of the individual's existence and, as such, is termed secular. Both music and religion, though, grapple in essence with the paradox of the finite being's attempt to become infinite. The composer with the greatest ability to transcend this paradox was Bach, whose works, sacred as well as secular, are suffused both with piety and a deep respect for the individual.

In the West-Eastern Divan the universal metaphysical language of music becomes the link that these young people have with each other; it is a language of continuous dialogue. Music is the common framework—an abstract language of harmony in contrast to the many other languages spoken in the orchestra—which makes it possible to express what is difficult or even forbidden to express with words. In music, nothing is independent. It requires a perfect balance between intellect, emotion and temperament. I would go so far as to argue that if this equilibrium were reached, human beings and even nations would be able to interact with each other with greater ease. Through music it is possible to imagine an alternative social model, where Utopia and practicality join forces, allowing us to express ourselves freely and hear each other's preoccupations. This model allows us to gain an insight into the way the world can, should and sometimes does in fact function. It was our belief from the beginning that the destinies of our two people—the Palestinians and the Israelis—are inextricably linked, and that therefore the welfare, the dignity and the happiness of one must inevitably be that of the other. This, unfortunately, is far from the way the situation is seen in the Middle East today.

The first session of the West-Eastern Divan Orchestra in Weimar had been financed by the European Capitals of Culture programme. In the following year, 2000, Bernd Kauffmann, who had been the director of the Weimar Capital of Culture in 1999, took it upon himself to look for funding in order for the project to continue, since it was clear that this could not be a unique event without repetition. That summer the project was visited by members of the board of the Chicago Symphony Orchestra, who were so taken by it that they committed themselves to hosting the orchestra the following year in Chicago. This had the great advantage that the young musicians—some of whom had never heard a professional symphony orchestra live before, let alone one of the world's greatest—would have the opportunity to hear the Chicago Symphony Orchestra rehearse and perform at its summer home in Ravinia, South Dakota. As the year progressed, the political situation between Israel and Palestine deteriorated further, eventually leading to the second Intifada. In addition there was no clear option for the project's location in the immediate future. For these reasons Edward Said and I even toyed with the idea of letting it rest for one year, but that carried with it the danger that the momentum that had been accumulating over two years would be lost.

In December 2001 I received a visit from Bernardino Leon, who was at the time the director of the Foundation for Three Cultures in Spain. The purpose of this foundation, as its name suggests, is the exchange of culture not just between the three religions of Judaism, Christianity and Islam, but between the three civilizations associated with each. Bernardino Leon arrived in Chicago with a proposal to continue the project in Seville. In our discussions Edward Said and I often came back to the fact that Muslims, Jews and Christians had lived in harmony only once in history: for seven centuries in Andalusia. Therefore the suggestion to go to Seville met with immediate enthusiasm on both our parts and in 2002 the workshop took place there. It had always been our policy in Weimar and Chicago to invite local musicians to participate in the orchestra—Germans and Americans who were interested in the project—which gave it a sense of belonging to each respective place and not merely existing as a foreign body in an anonymous setting. When we arrived in Andalusia, we realized just how fitting this place was to the project; the Andalusians had centuries of history in common with the Jews and Arabs, and therefore the project was particularly close to their hearts. Manuel Chavez, the President of the region of Andalusia, then offered to provide a permanent home for the workshop, a decision that was by no means an enterprise that would yield political dividends. When I asked him why he was nevertheless such a fervent supporter of the project, his answer was that Spain in general (and Andalusia in particular) is today what it is thanks to the fact that Jews and Muslims coexisted there for so many years, thereby contributing to the development of the country and its culture. If there were some way for Andalusia to give back today something of what it had received from these people over centuries, he felt it was not only his duty but a privilege to be able to do so. Edward and I were very impressed by his visionary way of thinking.

One of the most visibly evident traces of the mutual inspiration and influence of the three cultures is the decorative Mudéjar art present in many palaces, churches and synagogues throughout Andalusia. The word "Mudéjar" is derived from the Arabic *mudajjan*, meaning "those permitted to remain": in other words, the Muslims who submitted to the rule of the Christian kings, who in turn were so captivated by the intricate carvings, tiles and ceramics in Arab palaces and mosques that they hired the same artisans to construct and decorate their own palaces and churches. There is a common aesthetic shared by a great number of the sacred and secular structures of all the cultures of this period; the same Islamic motifs and patterns were adapted to the Christian cross and the star of David. Now, in the very same region, many centuries later, the musicians of the West-Eastern Divan Orchestra were being given the opportunity to re-create, in miniature, this creative exchange, using the structure of Western classical music as their common aesthetic.

In addition to the deep symbolic significance of bringing the orchestra to Andalusia, the rehearsal location and living quarters for the young musicians were ideal. The Lantana hostel in Pilas, about forty kilometers from Seville, combines the atmosphere of a university campus with that of a very pleasant retreat. It was once, in fact, a monastery and the lodgings are simple but more than adequate. There is an Olympic-size swimming pool where the musicians can retreat from the scorching heat of Andalusia (and Beethoven!) in August, and between the buildings that contain rehearsal rooms, cafeteria and dormitories there are lush green lawns that often become the site of discussions, debates, or just ordinary celebrations into the early hours of the morning. Rehearsals take place throughout the day in Pilas and private instruction by members of the Staatskapelle Berlin continue for as long as is necessary for each musician to make the greatest possible contribution to the orchestra regardless of his or her previous musical training or experience. It has been a source of great pleasure and pride for me that the musicians of the Staatskapelle have become so involved in the project that they treat it as their own. This involvement is by no means self-evident on the part of German musicians, for whom the Israeli–Palestinian conflict was but a mere item they read about in the newspapers. They are completely dedicated and spare themselves no effort to guide our young players in a way of making music that is very close to my heart. The discrepancy between the highest and lowest levels of proficiency and experience among the orchestra members has grown tremendously over the years. In the beginning, all the musicians were students, ranging in age from fourteen to mid-twenties, who displayed unusual musical talent, but many of whom had not had the training required to become professional musicians. Over the years, with the support of the teachers associated with the project and with the help of scholarships for study abroad, some of these students have joined orchestras such as the Damascus Symphony, the Israel Philharmonic, the Cairo Symphony and even the Berlin Philharmonic. The concert-master and the principal double bass of the Berlin Philharmonic (an Israeli and an Egyptian) and the principal timpanist of the Israel Philharmonic are members of the Divan Orchestra, and they sometimes sit together in the same section with students who have been playing their instruments for only two or three years. It is a magnificient opportunity for the students, and an act of generosity and dedication to the cause of the orchestra on the part of the professionals. After all, the project does not exist simply in order for the orchestra to play concerts; the professionals who continue to return to the orchestra do so not just because of the musical aspects but because of the humanitarian way of dealing with the conflict, which is also their own.

The West-Eastern Divan Orchestra is, of course, unable to bring about peace. It can, however, create the conditions for understanding without which it is impossible even to speak of peace. It has the potential to awaken the curiosity of each individual to listen to the narrative of the other and to inspire the courage necessary to hear what one would prefer to block out. Then, having heard the unacceptable, it may become possible at the very least to accept the legitimacy of the other's point of view. People have often called this a wonderful example of tolerance, a term I dislike, because to tolerate something or somebody implies an underlying negativity; one is tolerant in spite of certain negative qualities. The meaning of the word tolerance is misused when understood only as an aspect of altruistic generosity. There is an element of presumptuousness—I better than thou—inherent in it. Goethe expressed this succinctly when he said: "To merely tolerate is to insult; true liberalism means acceptance." True acceptance, I might add, means to acknowledge the difference and dignity of the other. In music, this is represented perfectly by counterpoint or polyphony. Acceptance of the freedom and individuality of the other is one of music's most important lessons.

The French Revolution, as I have said, gave us three lofty and truthful concepts—liberty, equality, fraternity. These ideals not only express the aspirations of the human being but are also articulated in a logical order. It is impossible to have equality without liberty and it certainly is impossible to have fraternity without equality. Music, evolving in time, demonstrates that the order of appearance of the material inevitably determines the content as well as its perception. The young musicians from the Middle East have the freedom of choice over whether or not to come to the West-Eastern Divan workshop. They know that in coming they will experience the equality that is denied them at home. There are a multitude of conditions that create equality within the orchestra and that can, with personal discipline, be carried over into civilian life. When applied on a personal level, these conditions help to change, if not the political reality, then at least the individual's perspective, which is both the smallest and perhaps most effective way to change the general approach to the conflict.

As Edward Said wrote, "My friend Daniel Barenboim and I have chosen this course for humanistic rather than political reasons, on the assumption that ignorance is not a strategy for sustainable survival." When Palestinians and other Arabs come together with Israelis to make music, the primary element that is lacking in the politics of the region, namely equality, is already a given. This equality may just be the starting point from which to contemplate the prerequisites for coexistence, the first one being the ability to understand the other's history, preoccupations, and needs for existence and development. Music, in this case the orchestra, is not an alternative solution, but rather a model. The diversity of the group lends itself to the peaceful coexistence of various national identities and, beyond that, to the liberation of each one's preconceptions about the others. This is one reason why it was possible for the West-Eastern Divan Orchestra to perform the Prelude and Liebestod from *Tristan und Isolde* by Wagner in Spain, Italy, Latin America, Great Britain and even in Germany. It would have been unthinkable for the Israeli members of the orchestra to do so in an exclusively Israeli orchestra, since the taboo on Wagner's music weighs heavily on their shoulders. This small example of defiance shows very clearly that the character of the project is more humanistic than political.

Wagner is a composer of such significance that these young Israelis were eager to play his music despite the negative associations with it and the abhorrent statements Wagner himself made about Jews and, in particular, Jews in music, as in the title of the notorious pamphlet that he published in 1850, at first under a pseudonym and then, ten years later, under his own name. At the time, it was part of the psychological make-up of a European nationalist (not only of a German one) to be anti-Semitic. Despite the power, money and influence Jews held in European society, they were treated as second-class citizens. The essence of European anti-Semitism in the nineteenth century was based on the fact that the Jews always remained a foreign body, no matter how much they tried to assimilate. Wagner was not exceptional in his anti-Semitism, he was simply exceptionally thorough and precise in articulating his racist sentiments.

When Hitler came to power he appropriated Wagner's writings about German art and German values—a term absurd in itself, since no nation can lay claim to any particular values over any other nation—and identified strongly with the heroic figure in his opera *Rienzi*, as someone who would liberate Germans from the influence of all foreigners. His affinity for Wagner went so far that, in some concentration camps, recordings of his music were performed as Jews were sent to the gas chambers. On the other hand, in the camps where prisoners were allowed to play in orchestras for the Nazi officers, they were forbidden to perform Wagner, because his music was deemed too good for the Jews. Thus the atrocities that have come to be associated with Wagner's music are vast and for some inseparable from it.

The discrepancy between the genius of his music and the despicable nature of his ideas about Jews is so overwhelming that Wagner has been the subject of hundreds of books. Without dedicating an entire volume to him, it must be said nevertheless that Wagner is an essential piece of the puzzle of music history. There are different criteria in determining the importance of composers: on the one hand there is the simple question of the merit or beauty of a body of work, and on the other its position in the development of music within history. We would undoubtedly be much poorer without the music of Mendelssohn, his violin concerto, *Songs Without Words*, octet and many other works. The beauty and perfection of his music is obvious and beyond all criticism, but the history of music would have developed in much the same way if Mendelssohn had not existed. Liszt, on the other hand, a composer of genius but perhaps lacking the craftsmanship and perfection of Mendelssohn, influenced tangibly and forcefully the path that music was to take; Berlioz represents a similar case. The influence of these two composers on Richard Wagner is impossible to overestimate and we know that without Wagner there would have been no Bruckner, Strauss, Mahler, or Schoenberg. There are only a handful of composers who summarize, and encapsulate, the entire period of composition until their time, while at the same time showing the path to the future, and Richard Wagner is certainly one of these. As with every important decision that is made in the orchestra, there was a vote to determine whether we would play Wagner or not. Only a few people objected, and since the orchestra is a democratic society, it was decided that we would play it; the result was an overwhelmingly powerful experience for everyone involved. The following summer the German mezzo-soprano Waltraud Meier was with us in Pilas, to participate in the activities of the orchestra and to rehearse the Ninth Symphony of Beethoven, which she performed with us five times that summer. On the afternoon of her arrival I told her to warm up her voice before the orchestra rehearsal because we had a surprise for her. She had been expecting to hear us rehearse the first Brahms Symphony, which was also on the program for the concert tour, and she could hardly contain her curiosity. When she heard the opening of the prelude to *Tristan und Isolde* she was visibly moved; and although the rehearsal room was full of visitors interested in the program and a few journalists—an audience of sorts—she stood with her back to them, facing the orchestra, as she began to sing the Liebestod. All of us—Waltraud, the orchestra and I—were moved by the experience. To hear this wonderful German singer communicate with Arabs and Israelis through the music of Wagner was to release the grip of so many oppressive spirits, so many taboos at once. Music, especially in the West-Eastern Divan Orchestra, is not simply a common activity that brings people together so that they might forget their differences; rather, it guides them to understand these very differences. It is an existential process that encourages reflection and understanding, helping us to delve beneath the surface and connect us to the source of our being.

Every conflict has the potential to bring about positive changes if the individuals involved in it are able to understand the legitimacy of the opposing side's arguments, sometimes even allowing these arguments to enhance their own way of thinking. The orchestra was put to a great test when, in 2004, the opportunity arose to play a concert in Ramallah. I had played recitals in Ramallah and at Birzeit University since 1999, and my own trepidation of bringing the Divan Orchestra to Ramallah made me very sympathetic to the fears and concerns of the young people who were considering this very courageous step, especially since many of them had never been to Palestine. There was much discussion about the decision to go, but then, finally, the tension that had mounted during the debate was dissipated when it was deemed too great a security risk for the orchestra to travel to Ramallah that year. The following year, however, I was fully determined to realize what could become for all of us an event of historic dimensions: a concert of an orchestra consisting of Palestinians, Israelis, Syrians, Lebanese, Egyptians and Jordanians in the heart of Palestine. It was truly an impossible undertaking and until the last moment it was doubtful that the concert would take place.

My primary concern, of course, was for the security of the musicians. It was forbidden by Israeli law for Israelis to venture into Palestinian territory, and it was forbidden by Syrian and Lebanese law for their subjects to go through Israeli territory, which was essential in order to reach Ramallah. The only two countries whose citizens could go legally were Egypt and Jordan, whose formal peace treaties with Israel can best be described as ice-cold. I was determined not to go through with the concert if there were any doubts about the safety of the journey or of the performance itself. Some of the Israelis had served in the army or were even still enrolled in the military at the time and were uneasy about going there; others were hesitant. Many musicians from the other Arab countries were unwilling to go to Palestine if they had to go through Israel and Israeli checkpoints to get there. Some of the Spanish musicians were simply afraid. The decision to go, in the end, touched a central nerve of the entire Israeli–Palestinian conflict, raising the issues of security, national identity, fear and all the preconceptions of the other party that make political progress so difficult.

The Spanish government, in a visionary and at the same time practical step, very generously offered to provide all the musicians of the orchestra with Spanish diplomatic passports valid for the duration of the trip. This only partly solved the formal problem, since all governments concerned were all perfectly aware of the legitimate citizenship of each traveling musician. This very diplomatic solution only reduced the musicians' individual anguish or fear of the trip itself and the consequences thereafter in their countries of origin. The Spanish government made it clear that it would assume responsibility for any eventual difficulties encountered by the musicians upon their return home, but this merely provided a limited release of tension for the individuals. We had been traveling since the beginning of August 2005, performing in Spain, Brazil, Uruguay, Argentina, at the Proms in London and the Edinburgh Festival. Throughout this tour, there were endless and sometimes in terminable discussions about all the aspects and ramifications of a trip to Ramallah. Bernardino Leon, now Spain's Secretary of State for Foreign Affairs, came to Brazil and participated in discussions with the orchestra, trying to calm the spirits. Fear, curiosity, courage, lack of trust and an undeniable sense of adventure mingled in the musicians' hearts; these strong emotions filled every day with excitement and desperation. In spite of the richness of the emotions and the high pitch of excitement, though, there was a mutual ever-present respect among the musicians. There was a vote, which decided by a vast majority to go to Ramallah, but it was clear that no one would be forced to go. There were only very few musicians who decided not to take part in the adventure, and those who did take part did so willingly and with full knowledge of the risks involved. The question remained, however, whether some of the members would be allowed by their governments to go.

On August 18, 2005 we played in the Rheingau Festival in Wiesbaden and it was already very late into the night before we were able to confirm that we had an orchestra to go to Ramallah. The day had started with some of the musicians still being uncertain about their governments' position on the question of travel to Palestine. Spain's former President, Felipe Gonzalez, and the Foreign Minister, Miguel Ángel Moratinos, played an active role in many ways, including forwarding all the necessary information to the governments in question. After they had received a very diplomatic message saying, in fact, that there would be no governmental objection, the musicians themselves reconfirmed this fact through their own contacts, and their final decision was taken but half an hour before the beginning of the concert in Wiesbaden. Some individuals were still undecided after the concert. Throughout the day there had been undeniable pressure on many of the Israelis from their families, while some of the Spanish musicians were reminded that this was primarily an Israeli-Arab project with a Spanish contribution and questioned whether it was imperative for them to go. One of them, a principal player, gave his final negative answer at midnight. At that late hour Tabaré Perlas, the manager of the orchestra, secured the participation of a member of the Staatskapelle who was in Berlin and was prepared to fly to Tel Aviv the next day, only to be told at 1:30 in the morning by the player who had originally opted out that he could not deny himself such an adventure.

On the following day the orchestra separated into different groups for security reasons. These young people had spent the summer together, sharing living quarters, meals, music stands and playing unforgettable concerts together. Splitting the orchestra into national groups, then, was a sobering moment for them, one that made them realize more than ever the importance and gravity of the situation. On August 19, the Israeli and Spanish musicians boarded a plane to Tel Aviv. The Spanish citizens continued immediately to Ramallah, the Israelis remaining in Israel until it was absolutely necessary for them to cross the border into the West Bank for the rehearsal and concert. Upon our arrival in Tel Aviv airport, I was met by a group of parents of the Israeli musicians; some of them had come to tell me how proud they were that their children were participating in such a unique occasion, but others questioned my right to take what was, in their minds, an irresponsible and dangerous step, even though their children were of age. I tried to reason with all concerned, but what actually convinced them was the fact that my own son would be leading the orchestra. This was undoubtedly one of the most difficult moments of my life; it was made bearable only after the fact by the historic event that we created there.

The Arab musicians boarded a plane to Amman in order to enter the West Bank from the Jordanian side. They arrived in Ramallah with Mariam Said, Edward's widow, on August 20, full of awe at the reality of being allowed to go to Palestine for the first time. Their excitement, however, was muted by the possibility of last-minute obstacles impeding the passage of the other half of the orchestra from Israel to the West Bank, in itself an illegal step. For security reasons, even the orchestra members were not told the specific time of the Israelis' arrival, heightening the already considerable suspense of waiting. Finally, early on the morning of August 21, the Israeli musicians were packed into bulletproof German diplomatic cars in Jerusalem and, after crossing the checkpoints, were escorted by Palestinian police to the Cultural Palace in Ramallah, where they were reunited with their colleagues in a atmosphere of elation. In this moment I was reminded once again that the impossible is sometimes easier to achieve than the difficult. It was scarcely believable that everyone was actually there in Ramallah in full concert dress, ready to rehearse and play a concert as if it were taking place anywhere in the world.

Mustafa Barghouti, an old friend of Edward Said's and co-founder with him of the Palestinian National Initiative, then Minister of Information of the Palestinian government, welcomed the orchestra and expressed his gratitude for the musicians' trust in himself, me, and all the Palestinians who were responsible for the organization of the trip. He was aware of all the trepidation and hesitation in the players' minds, and rightly understood that his personal involvement had greatly contributed to their decision to go to Ramallah.

Palestinian public reaction to the concert was divided between those who understood the depth of the message brought to them by the orchestra's performance there—this was the great majority—and those who were blinded by the idea that this might represent a normalization of the situation; in other words, an acceptance of the occupation. The former saw our coming as a model of the equality that might be achieved between Israel and Palestine, as was expressed in the music-making of these young people; the latter, unfortunately, could not hear and see Israelis and Palestinians playing together as long as Israeli tanks and soldiers were still present on the outskirts of Ramallah. For them, progress is impossible, or at the very least greatly hindered by the expectation that certain requirements be met before a dialogue can begin, even between civilians. In this case, both the symbolism of the orchestra and its potential to transcend one group's notions of the other are lost. This is indeed a great shame, as music does not distinguish between race, sex, religion, or place of origin. Before a Beethoven symphony all people are equal and can learn from it or be inspired by it, according to each person's capacity and willingness to do so. As far as fraternity is concerned, it is not an inevitable consequence of music, but the conditions for its development are present, which is not something one can say about the Middle East today. In any event, the concert was a triumph and for many an historic occasion. The Israelis, not having been allowed to leave the premises of the Cultural Palace throughout the day—this had been a joint stipulation of the Israeli and Palestinian authorities—were required to return to Israel as soon as the performance was over, even before the public left the concert hall. The irony of it all lay in the impossibility of the idea on the one hand and the ease of its physical implementation on the other. The Arabs and Spanish celebrated joyously throughout the night before returning to their countries the next morning. All concerned looked forward to the following year's reunion, without an inkling that a terrible cloud would descend upon all of us in the summer of 2006 in the form of the senseless, cruel war between Hizbollah and Israel.

In 2006, some of the Arab musicians were not allowed to take part in the orchestra in 2006 even if they had wanted to; others felt it was inappropriate to play music at a time of great suffering since, in their societies, music is regarded primarily as a pleasurable occupation; others still were uncomfortable with the idea of spending time together with the Israelis. This was of course, especially true of the Lebanese and Syrian members, who at the time were not able to leave their countries or had great difficulty doing so unless they had dual citizenship elsewhere as well and could board the ships or airplanes provided by those countries for fleeing refugees. Nevertheless, the workshop continued with the Israeli, Palestinian, Jordanian and some Egyptian musicians. The success of the project in 2006 must be judged by the fact that there were no defections among the members who came, rather than by the fact that some did not come at all.

One Lebanese violinist who also had Swiss citizenship arrived late, exhausted and devastated after a harrowing journey of several days, but she promptly attended rehearsal, attempting, like most of the others, to find an oasis of normalcy and a semblance of the ordinary continuation of life amid the violence and brutality of war. One had the feeling, throughout the period before the ceasefire was declared, that discussion of the events taking place was neither necessary nor possible. It was a time to immerse ourselves completely in the music, choosing to exist for the duration of the war in the infinite realm of musical expression in order to endure the finite pain felt by so many suffering civilians. Reality, however, kept reappearing, and Mariam Said and I felt it was impossible to appear in public at a time of war without making a clear statement about our beliefs. We therefore proposed a text to be printed in the concert programmes, the approval of which was brought to a vote and accepted by all but a handful of the orchestra members. The paragraph that applied to the war read as follows:

> This year, our project stands in sharp contrast to the cruelty and savagery that denies so many innocent civilians the possibility to continue living, fulfilling their ideals and dreams. The Israeli government's destruction of life-giving infrastructure in Lebanon and Gaza, uprooting a million people and inflicting heavy casualties on civilians, and Hezbollah's indiscriminate shelling of civilians in northern Israel are in total opposition to what we believe in. The refusal to have an immediate ceasefire and the refusal to enter into negotiations for resolving once and for all the conflict in all its aspects goes against the very essence of our project as well.

The year 2006 ended with an unforgettable performance on December 18, in the General Assembly Hall of the United Nations as part of the farewell ceremony for outgoing UN secretary-general Kofi Annan. To my great joy the full orchestra was completely reunited; most of the Syrian and Lebanese musicians were willing and able to come, and their presence on stage together with the other Arabs and Israelis was not only important for the balance of the orchestra, but also made a powerful statement in the United Nations.

The Sovereign Independent Republic of the West-Eastern Divan, as I like to call it, believes that if any progress is to be made in the Israeli–Palestinian dispute, it will require both sides to speak sensitively and listen painfully. Many of its citizens hear the pain of the other side's narrative for the first time during the workshop, and this is inevitably a shock that also requires them to think about the past, and about the suffering that has continued over so many years. Israel undoubtedly has a right to exist; the Palestinian people undoubtedly have a right to a sovereign, legitimate state. Israel needs security; the Palestinians need equality and dignity. These necessities and rights can only be granted by the Israelis to the Palestinians and by the Palestinians to the Israelis. The Israeli army is very powerful and probably able to win a war against an Arab country, but is nevertheless incapable of providing Israel with the security that its citizens require. Israel's security, in the long term, will only be achieved through its acceptance by the Palestinians and other neighbors. Israel's occupation of Palestinian land is a hindrance to this goal and its end is long overdue. Unilateral decisions have proved to be disastrous; they are morally unacceptable and strategically counterproductive. Only honest and courageous negotiations between parties, whether involved directly or indirectly in the conflict, can lead to liveable conditions both for the Israelis and the Palestinians. Isolation of these parties will make them part of the problem, whereas inclusion will make them part of the solution. I have frequently been admired for certain initiatives, often with the added allusion to naïveté on my part. I question, however, whether it is not even more naïve to rely on a military solution that has not worked for sixty years. The past is but a transition to the present and the present a transition to the future; therefore, a violent and cruel present will inevitably lead to an even more violent and cruel future.

Every member of the West-Eastern Divan Orchestra, regardless of his or her origin, shows a remarkable amount of courage, understanding and vision by taking part in the workshop. I would like to think of them as pioneers in a new way of thinking for the Middle East.

5

A Tale of Two Palestinians

Ramzi Aburedwan and Saleem Abboud Ashkar are two young Palestinians whose lives were changed dramatically by music. Born in Bethlehem, Ramzi Aburedwan grew up in a refugee camp in Ramallah surrounded by walls and borders and a general hatred of the Israeli oppressors. As a child he was renowned for throwing stones at Israeli soldiers; he himself was witness to shootings in the street, sometimes of his own family members and friends. His brother and father had both been killed when he was very young, and rather than becoming afraid of going out in the street, Ramzi became passionately hungry for revenge. There is a picture of him as an eight-year-old boy—stone in hand, arm raised, aiming for a target beyond the photographer—that was enlarged and posted in the streets. He was a hero for the voiceless population. Even the mountains surrounding Ramallah, which his family used to visit when he was very young, became inaccessible to Palestinians when Israeli settlers placed a roadblock on the way to the wilderness. These outings into nature had been a source of joy for Ramzi and his brothers and sisters, who could play freely there, pick fruit and shout into the valley, waiting for their echoes to return from the other side. When he was nine years old this refuge from the daily violence of the Israeli occupation was no longer available to him and his family, and there was nothing to distract him from the desire for revenge.

Saleem Abboud was born to a family in Nazareth that had chosen to stay put in 1948 after the city became part of the state of Israel. The creation of Israel had brought great joy to the Jewish population, for whom it had immense historical significance; but, for the Arab population, it was the *Nakba*, or catastrophe. Saleem's grandfather wished and hoped that the state of Israel would be dissolved, that the Arabs would defend their territory and win it back. As time passed, though, it seemed less and less likely that this would ever happen. Nevertheless, it was important to Saleem's father to remain in his homeland to live and work. An engineer, he had received countless offers for exciting career opportunities in other countries, all of which he had refused on the grounds of his loyalty to the Palestinian cause. If the strongest members of the Palestinian community were to leave, he reasoned, there would be no one left to speak for the rights of the minority, no hope of ever gaining statehood. Saleem's family, unlike Ramzi's, was not physically isolated from the rest of the world and did not suffer from any lack of material necessities. Both Saleem's parents were well employed, and he and his brother Nabeel went to good schools. Unlike Ramzi, they were able to move freely within Israeli society and travel if they wished. The walls and boundaries in their lives were different, invisible, in a way more insidious because internalized.

Ramzi had never seen or heard a Western musical instrument as a child. His grandfather had often listened to Oriental music on the radio, and although wonderful symphony orchestras had existed in Palestine (including the Palestine Orchestra, which later became the Israel Philharmonic), his family had no knowledge of them. It was not until Ramzi was seventeen that he met a Jordanian musician at a friend's home and was serendipitously introduced to the Western family of orchestral stringed instruments. This man, in Jordan to give a workshop on all the stringed instruments, helped Ramzi pick one that suited him best. They both decided upon the viola and Ramzi resolved to try to learn to play it during the course of the month-long workshop, with the intention of putting it aside again later. After all, music really had no place in Palestinian society in Ramallah other than as a pleasant diversion when times were good. Music, according to Ramzi, was not something one studied—it was far too elite, foreign, removed from the difficulties of daily life. At the end of the month, though, Ramzi not only did not want to put the viola down, he had discovered a way to leave behind the hopelessness of the refugee camp, of the occupation—music became his opportunity to go beyond the walls, borders and roadblocks in his environment, both literally and figuratively.

As a girl, Saleem's mother had gone to a school run by French nuns, which had a piano. For her, the piano had always been a sentimental emblem of a nearly forgotten childhood and, although she never had any formal musical education, it remained an important symbol for her. When a great wave of immigrants came to Israel from the former Soviet Union in 1970, many of them bartered what they had for what they needed. One such immigrant happened to have a piano and a need for a pickup truck, and Saleem's father had an old truck that was in disrepair and could not be sold in good conscience, so they traded. The piano in the Abboud household went largely unnoticed except as a piece of furniture until 1982, when Saleem was six years old, during the time of Israel's Good Fence Policy, which allowed certain people from Lebanon to visit Israel. One day that year a distant relative appeared on their doorstep, an artist by profession who could also play the piano. Born in Palestine, he had been sent to Munich by his father in the 1920s when he was fifteen years old to study medicine or become an engineer, but his real desire was to become an artist. He enrolled himself in the Munich Academy of the Arts where, in addition to studying painting and architecture, he also learned to play the piano. Although he eventually married a German woman and had two children with her, he was forced to leave the country when Hitler rose to power. When he came back to Germany to search for them in 1948 he was unable to find them; upon returning to Palestine he found it transformed into the state of Israel. Unlike the Abbouds, he decided to emigrate to Lebanon. Now, decades later, in Saleem's house, he immediately sat down at the piano and began to play. Saleem's parents, who both worked, were grateful to have a babysitter for the children and Saleem became entranced by his distant relative, by the music he played and by the piano. It was at this point that he told his parents that he had to learn to play the piano himself.

In Ramallah, after the Jordanian musician left, Ramzi continued to spend hours with his viola every day, playing Oriental melodies that he knew by heart from listening to his grandfather's radio. Later the same year a group of musicians from an American chamber music festival came to Ramallah to perform and teach at the conservatory, now known as the Edward Said National Conservatory of Music. The chamber music concert they played was the first Ramzi had ever heard and his first experience of Western classical music. Oriental musicians, when playing in a group, always played the same melody together simultaneously; he was bewildered by the diversity of voices in this music—five different musicians, all playing different parts at the same time. Their visit was brief, but Peter Sulski, the violist of the ensemble, returned a few months later, paying all his own expenses, to teach Ramzi and one other Palestinian girl. He brought with him the festival director, who gave Ramzi a scholarship to attend the Apple Hill Chamber Music Center in New Hampshire that summer. Despite his enthusiasm for the viola, Ramzi continued to express his frustration with the occupation in a physical way, sometimes picking up a stone on the way to his viola lesson and smashing the window of a settler's car. The invitation to the American festival was his first opportunity to leave Ramallah and the first time he was given the chance to concentrate exclusively on music. Although he had been playing the viola for less than a year, he was able to perform the viola part in Mozart's G minor

Piano Quartet by the end of the month, with the help of all the members of the faculty. He was possessed by an urge to understand the music and develop the coordination necessary to play the viola; during the course of the festival he worked twelve hours a day.

For young Saleem, now driven by the deep desire to play the piano, the best choice for his early musical education was a Russian Jewish piano teacher in Haifa and with each subsequent milestone in his musical development he became more deeply entrenched within Israeli society. He took part in Israeli competitions for young people, played with Israeli musicians and benefited from an Israeli education. When he won prizes in Israeli competitions, there was always a voice in his head that said, "It's because you're a Palestinian and they are giving you preferential treatment," but when he did not win a prize there was another voice that said, "It's because you're a Palestinian and not an Israeli." Whatever the case, there was never a pure achievement; every recognition or rejection was colored by his being a Palestinian, or, as the Israelis prefer to call them, an Israeli Arab. When he was thirteen and his education and development had become laden with political significance, his parents decided to send him to the more neutral territory of England to study.

When Ramzi arrived at Apple Hill, he was so elated to be immersed in music and surrounded by musicians of many nationalities that he was seized by the idea of bringing as many Palestinian children as possible to such a festival. He wanted to share the world he had discovered, that allowed him to think outside the limitations of the Israeli-Palestinian conflict, and to transcend the political and social restrictions of his surroundings. He knew at the time that this wish was pure fantasy, but the desire to change the lives of Palestinian children as his life had been changed was real, and in the following years he proceeded to realize the dream of opening a music school in Ramallah, with much help from the outside. Not long after returning from the

American festival he was given a scholarship to study at the Conservatoire de Musique in Angers, France for a year. One year led to another and, when he was not given a scholarship for a third year, he began to teach and play Oriental music to make a living while continuing to study. During the many years he had spent listening to Arab music in Ramallah he had never picked up an Arab instrument like the oud or the bouzouki, but now, in France, it became a way to finance his study of Western music. Originally sent to France as an exchange student, Ramzi fulfilled more than his end of the bargain, enriching the musical life of the conservatory with Middle Eastern harmonies. He taught a French singer and a French clarinet student some of the Arabic spoken and musical language and, together with another Palestinian percussionist, they formed an ensemble, Dalouna, that still performs all over Europe today.

Saleem was much less content than Ramzi to be away from home and family in London at the Yehudi Menuhin School. For one thing, the food was wretchedly inedible, especially in comparison to his mother's unparalleled Arabic cuisine. The high society of England, too, was an unpleasant contrast to the down-to-earth, generally socialist mentality of Israel. He returned after only three-quarters of a year to enroll in the Israeli Arts and Science Academy in Jerusalem, which was determined to be the first of its kind not only in its emphasis on the study of art and science but also in its openness to and inclusion of Palestinians. It was a mixed blessing for a Palestinian boy from Nazareth to be given a scholarship to study at an Israeli boarding school; he received all the benefits of an undoubtedly superior education but at the same time he was cut off from his roots, from his Palestinian identity. Although his family was by no means unconscious of the problem of this lack of a Palestinian identity, it was not until much later that Saleem began to confront the personal conflict of being part of an oppressed minority in his own land, a land that had been his ancestors' home for thousands of years. Without noticing it,

Saleem was in danger of becoming culturally disconnected from his own roots by virtue of his admittedly excellent Israeli education which, despite its high quality, omitted the study of any subject relevant to contemporary Palestinians. To include the study of these subjects would be equivalent to putting the Palestinian people on the cultural map of Israel, an act that would contradict Israel's Jewish identity.

After studying in France for seven years, Ramzi returned to Ramallah in 2002 to experience a kind of reverse culture shock. The Oslo Accords were now no more than a bitter memory and the future looked darker than ever. The development of children in Ramallah seemed the photographic negative image of the development of French children in Angers. There, the schoolrooms were decorated by the colorful artwork of children—pictures of houses, trees, animals, bright yellow suns—whereas the children in Ramallah, reflecting the objects in their own environment, were drawing pictures of tanks, machine guns, suicide bombers. This was an unacceptable, disastrous situation for a young man whose inner and outer life had been transformed by music. For him, the ability to produce his own sound on a musical instrument and the emotional and intellectual understanding necessary to grasp a piece of music had been central to his transformation as a human being. No longer the angry child throwing stones at his oppressors, Ramzi's first priority now was to touch the lives of as many children as possible. His first physical contact with a musical instrument had changed his life, and he began to play for children whenever he could. One day, after playing for a group of children, he noticed that they were attempting to draw his viola and, in a moment of simple but profound realization, he saw how easy it was to shape the thinking of a child, to change the contents of its consciousness.

With the help of friends from France whom he had met on the world music scene, he created a non-profit association to collect money for the cause and organized a day of benefit concerts of

"musicians for Palestine." Students from the conservatory in
Angers, eager to help, paid their own way to Palestine and were
fed and housed by Ramzi's family while they traveled all over the
West Bank gathering up groups of children and teaching them in
spontaneous workshops. Each time they came they remained for
several weeks, giving as many as fifty workshops and visiting
thousands of children; in total there were seven such tours
throughout Palestine, and sometimes the teachers ventured as
far as Gaza and Hebron.

When Ramzi speaks of living conditions in Ramallah today
and the dearth of cultural and intellectual life in Palestinian
society, there is a fire in his eyes, but it is no longer the wild fire of
hatred that once fueled his vengeful attitude; it has become a
controlled flame, fueling the creation of cultural nourishment for
young Palestinians. After the outburst of workshop tours, Ramzi
began to seek a permanent center for his musical and educational
activities, and with the help of a Palestinian cultural society he
found a ruin in the old city of Ramallah that could be renovated
with financial support from the Swedish government. During the
next eighteen months, Ramzi sought and finally gained permis-
sion from dozens of former owners of the building in order to
make it into a music school. Al Kamandjati, as he called it,
meaning "the violinist" in Arabic, has since become a flourishing
community center where 150 children have music lessons every
week. Throughout the period of its construction, he received
numerous donations of musical instruments from many European
countries as a result of flyers he had begun to distribute at each
performance of his Oriental music ensemble. Ironically, it was the
presence of Israeli settlers that brought some of the instruments to
Palestine, though indirectly. Every October during the olive
harvest, volunteers fly in from around the world to assist the
Palestinian people in collecting olives from the trees surrounding
the settlements (some of which had been established in the middle
of an olive grove) against the will of the settlers, who do

everything to prevent them from approaching the trees. The international volunteers were able to harvest the olives safely together with the Palestinians by making themselves plainly visible as foreigners. During the meeting of a French association for aid to Palestine at which his music school was discussed, Ramzi heard about the transportation of fifty French olive harvest volunteers to Palestine and, seizing the opportunity, arranged for each of them to carry one or two instruments on the journey to Palestine. In this way the volunteers did their part not only for the Palestinian economy, but for its cultural life as well.

Ramzi's urgency to bring Western music to Palestinian children grew out of his own existential need for it, and that need drove him to seek an education—and therefore also a perspective—beyond the physical boundaries that had confined him since birth. The boundaries in Saleem's life existed in much subtler form and became apparent to him only much later, when he began to notice his lack of connection to any culture that could be called purely Palestinian. It was his participation in the West-Eastern Divan Orchestra from its inception in 1998 that brought him into contact not only with Palestinians from the occupied territories but also, for the first time in his life, with other Arabs from Syria, Egypt, Jordan and Lebanon. Edward Said played a major role in awakening Saleem's awareness of his Palestinian heritage and of the necessity to view the Israeli contribution to his development not only with gratitude but also with a critical eye. Both Saleem and Ramzi come from islands of a sort; they were both denied the continuation of a history of their own and both come from a peculiar sort of oppressed minority. Their minority is unlike any other in history. It cannot be compared with, for example, the Turks in Germany, who immigrated en masse in the 1950s during the German economic boom, or the northern Africans, who settled in France after the independence of Algeria. The ancestors of Saleem and Ramzi simply stayed where they were, where they had lived for centuries, and were made into a minority by the political events of the twentieth century.

Much of the world remains ignorant of the problem of the growing minority of Palestinians within Israel, a minority that feels it has a religious, philosophical and historical right to be there. The Israeli Declaration of Independence states that "the state of Israel will devote itself to the development of this country for the benefit of all its people; It will be founded on the principles of freedom, justice and peace, guided by the visions of the prophets of Israel; It will grant full equal, social and political rights to all its citizens regardless of differences of religious faith, race or sex; It will ensure freedom of religion, conscience, language, education and culture." It goes on to commit the Israeli government "to pursue peace and good relations with all neighboring states and people."

Saleem, telling of his Israeli education, laments the fact that the only Arab literature that was included in the curriculum was either Egyptian or from the pre-Islamic era; contemporary Palestinian literature might be too politicized and would in any case present the very difficult question of Palestinian identity, one the school was not prepared to confront. When Shulamit Aloni was Minister of Culture, she tried to remedy this attitude but her attempt was probably too little, too late. This "oversight" is actually symptomatic of the fear and mistrust that has guided Israeli strategy in dealing with its Palestinian minority, and which has resulted in generations of Israeli Palestinians who have a disjointed sense of their own history and no sense of engagement with the difficult questions in their lives. In a manner of speaking, they have been anaesthetized by comfort: unlike the families in the overflowing refugee camp the West Bank and Gaza, they have the same right to education as Jewish Israelis and share the same standard of living. Unlike the conditions in Ramallah, which breed violence and unrest, the conditions in the mixed Israeli cities—or, even more so, in a city like Nazareth, which has been divided—simply breed indifference and ignorance of the problem of a Palestinian identity among Palestinians and Israelis alike. Unlike Ramzi, who was confronted on a daily basis by his own need to avenge the injustice of his people's circumstances, Saleem remained long unaware that there was a problem to confront, being, as he was, a product of Israeli education, if not a fully participating member of its society.

Today, nearly sixty years after the creation of the state of Israel, the country finds itself at a crossroads; it is confronted at once with three fundamental problems: that of the nature of the modern democratic Jewish state—its very identity—and that of the Palestinian identity within Israel; and the possible creation of a Palestinian state. With Jordan and Egypt it was possible to attain at least a cold peace without threatening or questioning Israel's identity as a Jewish state. The problem of the Palestinians in Israel, though, is a much more challenging one to solve, both theoretically and practically. For Israel it means, among other things, coming to terms with the fact that the land was not barren, empty, an idea that was propagated at the time of its creation. For the displaced—or, in the case of those who remained, disconnected—Palestinians it means accepting the fact that Israel is a Jewish state, or, even worse from their point of view, a state for the Jews.

The creation of the state of Israel was not the beginning of antipathy between Arabs and Jews; the Arab population of Palestine had been unsympathetic toward Jewish immigration from the very beginning. After 1948, of course, the situation only deteriorated. The Jewish population had finally achieved statehood after thousands of years in the diaspora and the Arabs of the region had to choose whether to stay in a country in which they would become a frustrated minority, like Saleem's family, or to emigrate to one of the other Arab countries. In the past twenty years Israel's new historians have documented the fact that many did not even have these two choices, but were made to leave by force. There was a great deal of mistrust on both sides from the beginning of Israel's existence and at first the old Arab cities were subject to Israeli military rule. Even Saleem, as part of the Palestinian minority, can understand Israel's fear that its security was then at stake and that these measures, abominable as they were, were necessary for its self-preservation. Decades after the military threat had receded, though, the attitude remained; there was no real shift in the strategy of the Israeli government toward its non-Jewish citizens, no recognition that this group no longer posed an existential threat to the state. But Palestinians living in Israel today continue to be simply tolerated and not integrated into Israeli society. Saleem and his brother, who were able to participate in Israeli society, who were even supported and educated by the Israeli system, still remain, like all Palestinians, second-class citizens with no sense of belonging to the country in which they live.

Today, Palestinians make up nearly 22 percent of the population of Israel. This is a larger percentage than was ever represented by a Jewish minority in any country in any period of history. To consider the integration of such a large minority into the Jewish state is to shake the roots of the Jewish psyche, to challenge the notion of Jewish identity as it has developed over the centuries. The Jewish spirit must decide whether it felt at home or was always a foreign body in the diaspora. The question that subsequently arises is whether the need for the creation of a Jewish state arose only as a result of the persecution the Jews had been subject to through the centuries or whether the Jewish spirit had always yearned for a home of its own. If the latter is true, then one must examine the difference between the terms "home" and 'nationhood'. In fact, there are many nuances of this definition that differentiate between various ideas and ideals: a home for the Jews; a nation for the Jews; a Jewish state; a state for the Jews. Arthur James Balfour, the British Foreign Secretary wrote to Lord Rothschild in 1917: "His Majesty's Government view with favor the establishment in Palestine of a national *home* [italics mine] for the Jewish people, and will use their best endeavors to facilitate the achievement of this object, it being clearly understood that nothing shall be done which may prejudice the civil and religious rights of existing non-Jewish communities in Palestine, or the rights and political status enjoyed by Jews in any other country."

It bears remarking that the Zionist idea that gave birth to the state of Israel arrived, paradoxically, at a similar analysis of the Jewish problem in Europe as that of the anti-Semitic movement: namely, that the Jews had always been a foreign body and would remain so unless they abandoned their Jewishness. Assimilation had failed and integration was unacceptable to both parties. Wagner wrote in his pamphlet *Das Judentum in der Musik* (Judaism [first translated as] or Jewishness in Music), that the Jews were incapable of writing German music but nevertheless had such a significant cultural influence as to be damaging to the development of true German music. His conclusion—namely, that the Jews must disappear, either by emigration or by complete assimilation into German culture—is not far from the conclusion reached by the early Zionists. They saw the situation of the Jews in Europe not only as a social or religious problem but as a political one as well, and dedicated themselves to finding a political solution. If one extrapolates the dialectic thought process between the anti-Semites and the Zionists, one arrives at the creation of the state of Israel.

The Jews, now finally at home in Israel, must accept the integration of the Palestinian minority even if it means changing the very nature of Israel; not only is there no alternative, or magic wand, that will make the Palestinians disappear, but their integration is an indispensable condition—on moral, social and political grounds—for the survival of Israel. The longer Palestinian dissatisfaction remains unaddressed, the more difficult it will be to find the necessary common ground. Clearly, dissatisfaction, unhappiness and a feeling of injustice over a long period of time have had the effect of radicalizing their demands and weakening their acceptance of the tangible benefits of Israeli education, health care and other social boons. We have seen so often in the modern history of Israel that missed opportunities on both sides have had extremely negative results for both. We know from music that not only the speed, but also the timing of an event alters and sometimes even determines its direction and content. An unexpected modulation, for instance, would fail to introduce the intended element of surprise if it appeared too soon in a musical composition; in order to fit into the composition at all, though, it must arrive at a very precise moment when the development of the piece requires it. With the passage of time, the hardening of the Palestinian position on cultural, social and political issues makes their demands more difficult for Israel to accept. What would have been an act of generosity soon after the Six Day War in 1967, such as the return of occupied territories, will today, now that the necessity of doing so is internationally recognized, inevitably be construed as an unavoidable act of weakness on Israel's part. The fact that the whole Arab world was not willing to negotiate from a position of weakness should have inspired Israel to develop creative propositions rather than to solidify its unyielding attitude. I believe, however, that Israel has not yet been able to understand rationally its strength or weakness in the conflict and has consequently vacillated from one extreme to the other. The residue of having been persecuted and victimized throughout history may be an element that keeps it from objectively measuring its strength as a state.

Israel's attitude toward the Palestinians who live in the country has often catalyzed the disappearance of Palestinian identity and cultural roots. In the old Arab cities, in which many Arabs still live, streets that were named after Arab figures, some of them prehistoric, were either assigned anonymous numbers or renamed after Israeli generals who fought in the War of Independence. This seemingly small but symbolically significant change—at best thoughtlessness and insensitivity on the part of Israel and at worst an utter lack of strategy in dealing with the question of Arabs in Israel—is an example of Israel's denial of the simple fact that a percentage of the population of the area has always been non-Jewish. The Jewish population during the First World War represented a mere 15 percent of the total population of Palestine. Too often in the course of its short history, Israel has looked primarily to the recent past and to its Central and Eastern European Jewish roots to seek its identity and relationship to the world. How much wiser it would have been for all countries of the region to accept each other's existence and to look for the similarities between the two Semitic people rather than the differences. The centuries of peaceful coexistence between Jews and Muslims in Andalusia should be seen not only as an example from the distant past of the possibility of coexistence between these two peoples, but as proof of their capacity for mutual enhancement. The Andalusian medieval philosopher and rabbi Maimonides not only spoke and wrote in Arabic as well as in Hebrew, but was also part of a society that included both identities and cultures. How great an impact this society of multiple identities had on his philosophy can only be a point of speculation; it is not difficult to imagine, though, that his *Guide for the Perplexed* would have been different had he lived in a less diverse community.

The predicament of the Palestinians in Israel is in some ways even more devastating than that of the Marranos during the Spanish Inquisition; the Marranos were forced to convert to Christianity and treated as second-class citizens, but in secret they continued to practise Judaism, maintaining their identity and place within history. The Israeli Palestinians, on the other hand, have been educated in a system that has erased their people's cultural contribution and history from the curriculum. In the void of a healthy identity based on culture and history, a potentially dangerous religious movement has begun to take shape, one that is different from Hamas in the occupied territories, which was at one point supported by Israel in order to weaken Arafat and Fatah.

Hamas was born out of protest against two issues: the injustice the party feels was brought upon the Palestinians with the creation of Israel; and the existence of Palestinian secular corruption in their own government. The Israeli-Palestinian religious movement is different in that it is a direct result of the weakening of Palestinian identity within Israeli society. It is immaterial whether the responsibility for this situation is exclusively Israeli, exclusively Palestinian, or a combination of both; the fact remains that religion gives clear directives that replace the intellectual activity of questioning that accompanies logical analysis. Many people are unaware of the fact that the Palestinian population of Israel is also made up of Christians, for whom the new Islamic religious movement is meaningless; therefore, the division can only become greater. The Palestinian cultural void creates a vicious circle for both parties: Israel uses it to justify its second-class treatment of the Palestinians who, for their part, feel slighted by this attitude and have no motivation to want to belong to a state that does not treat them as equals.

The Palestinians feel that they have been victimized both by Israel and by the rest of the Arab world, which had promised to liberate Palestine from the Jews. For sixty years, now, they have been waiting for the creation of a Palestinian state. Although the Palestinians of Israel are divided by this question—some of them would not leave if a Palestinian state were created—they all agree that they cannot live in Israel as it is today. From an objective point of view this situation is a result of a lack of Israeli strategic thinking over the last forty years, which is now endangering its very existence as a Jewish state. The Palestinians perceive the same situation as immoral. Israel's national identity could be described as a fetus which, fully developed, has not yet been delivered, endangering its own life and that of the mother as well.

Even before the creation of a Jewish state and of all the problems of integration and acceptance that went with it, there was a movement among Jewish composers in Palestine in the 1930s and 1940s to integrate Middle Eastern melody, harmony and rhythms into their music. This movement was an attempt to create music with a Middle Eastern—or Oriental, as it was called in those days—flair. The followers of the movement achieved, quite intuitively, a musical flavor that reflects both Jewish and Arab characteristics. Paul Ben-Haim, the leader of the movement, was one such composer who instinctively realized a truth that politicians today have still not grasped, that the Israeli identity must include its geographical environment, of which the Arab element is an essential part. Born Paul Frankenburger in Munich in 1897, he studied composition, conducting and piano at the Munich Academy of the Arts from 1915 to 1920, not long before Saleem's relative would also study at the same academy.

Frankenburger served as assistant to Bruno Walter and Hans Knappertsbusch at the Munich Opera, and conducted in the Augsburg Opera from 1924 to 1931, but when the Nazis came to power in 1933 he emigrated to Palestine, changing his name to Ben-Haim. It was then that he began to experiment with the incorporation of Middle Eastern musical elements into his composition, although he had already written an Oratorio based on biblical themes while still in Germany. Making the best of the cultural isolation forced upon him and other musicians during World War Two, he conducted extensive research into Middle Eastern folk tunes and rhythms, weaving them into his own otherwise rather conservative late-Romantic style of composition. Perhaps this wartime isolation was partly responsible for the need among Jewish composers in Palestine to seek a new identity, which was not only influenced by, but even welcomed, the enhancement of local culture, an attitude strikingly absent from today's political discussions in the Middle East. This intuitive conclusion demonstrates that music can be much more than just a pleasurable ornamental element of culture; in this case it was far ahead of historical and political developments in society. The world of sound, it seems, is capable of elevating the individual from a limited preoccupation with his own existence to a universal perception of his place among fellow human beings.

Of the many political parties existing in Palestine at the time, the Communist Party was the only one that accepted the partition of Palestine, thereby accepting the existence of Israel. It was also the only party that included Arabs and Jews. The USSR, unsurprisingly, was the first country to acknowledge the state of Israel, partly because of Stalin's strategic interests, but also because of an affinity between the Russian nation and the Socialist movement in Israel. The kibbutz, which does not allow any private property, and the moshav, which is based on collective ownership, were both examples of what must have seemed to the Russians a realization of the socialist dream. Stalin realized very quickly that he had misjudged the political direction that Israel would take, and it was only after his death that the Soviet Union became an active player in the Middle Eastern world. After the Suez War of 1956, it was Gamal Abdel Nasser who obtained Soviet political and economic support for Egypt, thereby allowing the Cold War powers to participate actively in Middle Eastern politics.

In 1970, the Soviet Union opened its doors to allow Jewish immigration to Israel for the first time since the Second World War. These immigrants suffused Israel with new energy in its cultural, medical and technological realms. It was at this time that a generational change took place within the Israel Philharmonic, whose founders had come predominantly from Central Europe. Now they were replaced, for the most part, by the new Russian immigrants who inevitably changed the style of the orchestra. It is the only case in the history of music in which an orchestra changed its style so drastically. The advances in medical research and technology have been very well documented and were of enormous value to Israeli society, but this new injection of life did not come without its dangers. The Soviet Jewish immigrants had lived in political isolation; anti-Semitism in the Soviet Union had never disappeared. The combination of these two elements created a very nationalistic faction of new Israeli citizens, which had no interest whatsoever in the Palestinian problem.

Saleem's distant relative from Lebanon had appeared in 1982 with a stack of music in Russian editions—only later, at school, did Saleem understand that Haydn was not a Russian composer. Like Saleem's father, his piano-playing relative had also been a member of the Communist Party and had acquired his sheet music through connections to Moscow. The cultural influence of the Soviet Union and the Communist Party extended beyond Israel to Syria, Jordan and Egypt, ironically providing a basis for cultural unity where there was no political unity. Many Russian musicians performed and taught in these countries, and still do, with the result that many of the members of the West-Eastern Divan Orchestra, regardless of their origins, come from similar schools of playing.

The cultural wealth shared by the Israeli and Arabic peoples is staggering in its diversity and richness, yet it is necessary consciously to seek the similarities between the two in order to build a foundation that will support not a fence, but a forum for cooperation between the two populations. The paradox of the Israeli-Palestinian conflict is that it cannot be solved by the application of international axioms because of its local nature. On the other hand, though, the conflict, like an ancient olive tree, has developed many branches and scattered many seeds that, over time, have returned to grow into new problems, which must be addressed on both a local and a global level.

6

Finale

Music possesses a power that goes beyond words. It has the power to move us, and it has the sheer physical power of sound, which literally resonates within our bodies for the duration of its existence. The power that music has over us has often been the subject of literary and visual works of art, but rarely is it discussed in a rational, physical way. It is difficult to distinguish between the substance of music and the listener's perception of it. It is probably for this reason that music, since Homer's day, has sometimes been portrayed as a potential danger to the health of the intellect and even of the will; music was capable of everything from inducing states of Dionysian hallucination to seducing Odysseus and his entire crew away from the completion of their voyage. The educated ear, however, cultivates the ability to separate the content of the music from the feelings one has learned to associate with it.

Music is conceived by and eventually delivered from the point of view of an individual. As a result, subjectivity is an integral and inevitable part of music, although it is not the only one. While there is no such thing as an objective performance, there must be a permanent relationship between subjectivity and objectivity when making music, as there is in life. Even the freedom of speed in music, tempo rubato, cannot be wilfully conceived, but must be in contact with the underlying and uncompromising metronomic pulse (in other words tempo non rubato); it is precisely this constant connection between yielding and unyielding elements that gives the performance of music the richness of being simultaneously subjective and objective. With this notion we are once again confronted with what I would call the moral responsibility of the ear.

Because music only expresses itself through sound and takes place in a given time, it is, by its very nature, ephemeral. What is essential in the performance of music and difficult in life is the ability to start from nil each time. Every time one performs a work again, one must do so with the freshness of a first encounter and the intensity of a last one. It is very difficult to have the courage and ability to start from nothing, examining experience collected in the past and then beginning to think anew, in a different way. It is equally difficult to lend a new experience the effortless, natural qualities of an already familiar one.

I know of no other performing artists who turn their attention so intensely, and often exclusively, toward the past as classical musicians. Finding the music of the past to be timeless, universal and an unlimited source of inspiration, some musicians believe that by limiting themselves to a narrow selection of works from earlier centuries their understanding of them will attain greater depth. I believe, on the contrary, there is a need to be in touch or even abreast of contemporary music in order to keep one's curiosity constantly alive. The knowledge and performance of contemporary music enhances one's understanding of the masterpieces of the past. I have not only enjoyed conducting many works of Pierre Boulez and Elliott Carter, but have learned from this experience many important aspects of music making that proved very enlightening and useful when returning to Beethoven and Wagner. The exploration of the music of today may be considered different from that of the music of the past, in that it requires a greater effort to discover it, and then to develop individual preferences and tastes as one has toward earlier music. If this is done only out of a sense of duty to contemporary music, there can be no joy and no critical differentiation in seeking out works that are worthy of being performed with the great music of the past. The importance of a contemporary piece can best be appreciated when juxtaposed in the same program with, for example, a Beethoven symphony. My only criterion for new music—or any music, for that matter—is that, at the moment of performance, the composition must be the center of my interest and attention, eclipsing all other works while it lasts.

By artificially preserving the ephemeral, recordings have demonstrated the futility of recycling our musical ideas, simply reproducing an insight that has occurred to us at some previous point and continues to serve us as an unchanging and convenient vehicle for our performance of a certain work. A recording is a more perfect device than a human being for reproducing an interpretation that was the result of spontaneous comprehension; it is the human being's duty to find new and urgent truths in a work if he is to study and perform it more than once. Music loses its power when the performer loses his curiosity and humility before it.

It is crucial to distinguish between the nature of music on the one hand and the associations that it evokes on the other—yet another instance of the finite before the infinite. The nature of a great work encompasses as much of human nature, and human experience, as the intellect and talent of its creator allows. The movements or ways of thinking that come to be associated with such a work are entirely separate from the creative process and should never be confused with the spirit in which a work was conceived. Beethoven was both used and abused in German politics by Bismarck, Hitler and the former German Democratic Republic. Consider the irony of Beethoven's Ninth Symphony being played in the Nazi era: "*Alle Menschen werden Brüder*" (All men will become brothers). In other words, the Nazis annexed Beethoven's creative property, redefining his concept of fraternity to suit their own, which of course did not include all of humanity.

The distinction between music and the associations it evokes could be described more generally as the difference between substance and perception. Much too often, in our time, we attempt to alter the substance of something in order to suit its perception. When one plays a piece of music, one must free its essence of any extraneous meanings that have become attached to it, whether by one's own doing or through the influence of others. One such example is the obviously erroneous perception that Chopin's tuberculosis had a discernible influence on his music, which would require the pianist to perform it anaemically; another is the popular tendency to discuss Mahler's music not in musical terms but in a psychoanalytical context that explains its neuroses according to the theories of Sigmund Freud. Notwithstanding the benefits to be derived from a familiarity with a composer's life— in that it can give us a hint of the society in which he lived and his place in it—it is utterly senseless to use a composer's music simply to portray aspects of his biography.

No matter how objective the individual tries to be, there is inevitably an element of subjectivity involved; the boundaries between content and perception are not always easy to recognise, although they are always defined by the printed page. As I have already discussed, the use and abuse of Wagner's ideas and music were an integral part of the last years of the Third Reich—in fact, of the whole Third Reich. This regime was a master of the control and manipulation of perception. The Nazis' appropriation of Wagner's anti-Semitic prose transformed him retrospectively into the prophet of their ideology. It is not only understandable, but self-evident, that somebody who was submitted to this manipulation will still suffer today from these associations and is therefore not only unwilling but unable to hear this music.

Music is neither moral nor immoral. It is our reaction to it that makes it one or the other in our minds. Today's society sees controversy as a negative attribute. Yet difference of opinion and the difference between content and the perception of it lie at the very essence of all creativity. There is no reason in the world to force those who suffer from the associations between Wagner's music and Nazi ideology to listen to his music. In Israel, the general consensus is that it shows more sensitivity toward the survivors of the Holocaust to ban the performance of Wagner's music. In fact, there is no justification for depriving people who fortunately do not suffer from these horrible associations of the possibility to hear Wagner's music. Therefore, the refusal to let his music be heard today represents an acceptance of the associations created by the Nazis. In fact, it was performed at the very second concert of the Palestine Philharmonic Orchestra—today the Israel Philharmonic Orchestra—in Tel Aviv in 1936, when Wagner's anti-Semitism was already well known.

It is not my intention—it never was and never will be—to force this or any music on anybody, and I certainly do not question the horrible associations that Holocaust survivors have with specific pieces by Wagner. I can only hope that time will eventually help to liberate them from their associations with this music, so that ultimately they can hear it for what it truly is and not for what it has come to represent. It is not my place to tell those who suffered from terrible associations what to think of Wagner, but I believe it is important to tell those who are willing to listen to Wagner that the music in itself is not the agent of suffering. In the meantime, however, it is equally important not to impose negative associations, albeit indirectly, on those who fortunately do not suffer from them. In a democratic society the decision to permit or forbid the performance of music must be individual and not dictated by law or even worse, the result of a taboo. A law, at least, is the result of a thought process, whereas a taboo is the result of a collective subconscious feeling whose origin is often ignorance or fear. It is the individual's prerogative to choose between perceiving "Siegfried's Funeral March" as an expression of nobility or as a recollection of the connotations that Hitler wanted Wagner to have.

Returning to the difference between content and perception, we cannot avoid being influenced by content—Wagner's music—but it is in our power not to be influenced, let alone dominated, by perceptions—our associations. As Kant said, "If it were not for the distinction between appearances and things, we would all be Spinozists." We are slaves to the associations created by listening to music—like Odysseus—until we understand its substance. As we already know, although music may mean different things to different people, and very often different things to the same person at different times—poetical, mathematical, sensual, or philosophical—we must not forget that it only expresses itself through sound and that it touches all these realms at once and goes beyond them as well.

The beginning of a political process, in much the same way as the beginning of a musical phrase, sets something in motion that strives to have a life and a speed of its own. Living as dispersed minorities all over the world, the Jewish people aspired to nationhood and eventually the state of Israel was created in 1948. It was fraught with difficulties and rejected by the non-Jewish population in Palestine, but it persevered with the power of a leitmotif and was aided by the supporting voice of the world's conscience.

In the Israeli-Palestinian conflict there was and still is an inability to admit the interdependence of their two voices as well as the inevitable change brought about by time. The creation of the state of Israel was the result of a Jewish-European idea which, if it is to extend its leitmotif into the future, must accept the Palestinian identity as an equally valid one. The Palestinians hear Israel playing its theme in the wrong tonality and have aspirations to determine their own home key. Even the most powerful leitmotif, though, is dependent on the modulations that occur within it. The demographic changes taking place in Israel are impossible to ignore; the Palestinians both within and outside Israel need to be heard now more than ever.

If one could transcribe the Israeli-Palestinian dialogue into a great work of music, it would acquire the status and the distance it needs to be understood, appreciated and objectively felt by both parties. In a piece of music, the very fact that two or more voices exist simultaneously lends them both legitimacy, and in Western music there is no such thing as a one-sided narration; contrapuntal dialogue always presents at least two narratives at once and allows each to present itself fully but never to speak without a counterpart to support, contradict and complete its own statement. The Israeli and Palestinian narratives—their constant re-evaluations and rewritings of their own histories—exist in the same state of permanent interconnection as do the subject and countersubject of a fugue. Without the countersubject there is no fugue. One cannot say that the subject has more importance than the countersubject, since it is an objective reality that neither has any logical place without the other.

As subject and countersubject, it is essential for both peoples to understand not only their own narration, but also the human experience of the other. In a fugue, the subject does not have the luxury (or the misfortune) of hearing its own voice alone, again and again. It makes its statement once and when it repeats itself it shares the stage with the countersubject which, from then on, is a constant companion and a permanent reminder of all that the subject itself is not. Subject and countersubject complete each other and depend on one another for their existence in the world of sound. If the Israelis and Palestinians could see the parallel between their own dialogue—or lack thereof—and the structure of the fugue, they, too, would realize the urgency of coexisting.

Israel is losing its capacity to recollect; it only remembers. This, too, would be an impossibility in any musical form. When a theme has passed through all its modulations and developments, and makes its re-entrance in the recapitulation of sonata form, it is at that point the result of its entire experience, not simply of one event, regardless of how dramatic or important it may have been.

The Holocaust is, in historical terms, an episode. Obviously, as an episode of such abominable magnitude, it must be recognized and studied by the world, including the Palestinians, to prevent it from being repeated at any time in any place in the world. Edward Said understood this perfectly and fought against the stupidity and cruelty of the Holocaust deniers.

To deny the Holocaust or belittle its importance is not only stupid—because it opens the door to a repetition of the catastrophe—and cruel to the memory of those who perished and to the courage of those who survived; it is also immoral.

To say "never again" is both subjectively and objectively imperative; however, these words must be subjected to constant reflection. The words "never again" uttered without reflection can become a repetitive reflex which, although meant as a homage to those who suffered and perished, can also take on the quality of a slogan. This quality both diminishes the impact of these words and makes further discussion impossible, since a slogan, as we already know, is at the very least a deformation of the original idea. Deformation of the idea, in this case, can easily lead to a reliance on militaristic elements in society, which in turn ensure that the future will be dominated by fear as the past was.

During the time following Israel's founding as a state, the Holocaust was hardly present in public discourse; on the individual level it was understandably avoided by the survivors because of the pain it brought back, while the new generation wanted to dissociate itself at all costs from the image of the Jew as a victim. Therefore, both those who had experienced the Holocaust and those who fortunately only knew about it at one remove considered a discussion of the subject uncomfortable. The majority of young Israelis in the 1950s were concerned with creating an ideal society in which Zionism walked hand in hand with socialism (the kibbutz being a clear example). They wanted to live life in a collective, existential and just way. Eliminating the past from everyday thinking had the unfortunate result that not all the different aspects that contributed to the creation of the state were addressed. Ignoring the past meant ignoring the very existence of the non-Jewish population in Palestine.

The capture of Adolf Eichmann in Argentina in 1961 and the trial that followed in Jerusalem were not simply the process of bringing a criminal to justice—and what a criminal at that, having been one of the primary advocates and perpetrators of the "final solution"—it was also a necessary educational experience for the young generation in Israel precisely because the Holocaust had not been a topic of great urgency for well over a decade. It was the first time that the young population of Israel had been confronted with the full horror of the Holocaust. While it renewed the pain and suffering of the survivors, it also enabled them to open their hearts to the next generation. Broadcast live every day on television of the trial, the images of one of the worst criminals in history brought forth individual testimonies of the most horrific nature and a cynical defence by the accused, who claimed only to have been following orders. The terrible and constant presence of the trial made it impossible to continue to circumscribe the subject. If evil can be defined as the absence of thought, as Hannah Arendt wrote in her book *Eichmann in Jerusalem: A Report on the Banality of Evil*, then forgetfulness is a not-too-distant relative and this, too, was an important lesson for Israel's citizens. Thought and morality go hand in hand, and there can certainly be no morality without thought.

A sense of morality undoubtedly belongs to the Jewish people's historic capital and has allowed it to survive the most devastating forms of anti-Semitism. Israel is wasting this very capital by maintaining the occupation and creating settlements on land that does not belong to it. The preoccupation with moral standards was always at the root of Jewish thought throughout history; justice, rather than love (as in the Christian religion), was always at the center of Jewish religious thought. Israel's behavior since 1967, however, has allowed the Palestinians to feel morally stronger.

The horror of the Holocaust's inhumanity is even larger than the suffering it has brought to the Jewish people—the tragedy belongs to all humanity. When we, the Jews say "never again," it is often a reference to the necessity never to allow the same crime to be repeated against our own people, whereas the rest of the world has understood the same phrase to mean that this crime must never be repeated anywhere, at any time, against any people. I am convinced that the ability to see it as such is the only way Israel can gain the clarity of thought and emotional capacity necessary for its interactions with the Palestinians. If it is true that the Palestinians will not be able to accept Israel without accepting its history—including the Holocaust—it is equally true that Israel will not be able to accept the Palestinians as equals as long as the Holocaust is its *only* moral standard.

If Israel wants to have a permanent place in the Middle East it must become an organic part of it, being aware of the culture that already existed there and not pretending, as it has for too long, that it was a desert, barren of culture. To secure the future of Israel, it is necessary for Israelis to open their ears to Arab culture. This is not to say that Israel should deny its European roots, but rather that this very heritage would be enriched and enhanced by placing it side by side with its Middle Eastern heritage. If Israel remains closed to intellectual and cultural influence by its neighbours, it will remain a foreign body in the Middle East and this would have disastrous consequences for the longevity of the state; a foreign body can exist in a society, in music, or in a human being, only for a limited amount of time. This is very different from the question of assimilation, which the Jews had to face in Europe in order to survive or become full-fledged citizens; the fact that it is a state should encourage Israel to include other elements than those that were essential for its creation.

The genuine and original idea of the renewal of Jewish settlements in Palestine has been thwarted by factions that believe that forceful control, rather than what Martin Buber called the command of the spirit, rules the social and political destiny of humanity. This celebration of force has led to an insensitivity to and misunderstanding of the fact that the command of the spirit can only mean that this is a land for two peoples, with opposing narratives, but of equal rights. As Buber said, "There can be no peace between Jews and Arabs that is only a cessation of war; there can only be a peace of genuine cooperation."[1] In other words, peace requires dialogue, which consists of sensitive talking and often painful listening.

Leadership throughout history—and this is probably inherent in human nature—has been based on the effect it can produce because of the weakness of the people, not because of their strength; it has relied on the conformity of the individual to the collective rather than on the power to be derived from the individual contribution of each member of society. The age-old tradition of Jewish individualism that was partly responsible for establishing the state of Israel was ironically suppressed by the same mentality that sought to unite its citizens for the common good. Throughout the first half of the twentieth century, Jewish immigrants had arrived in Palestine with a vision that combined Zionism and Socialism, preferring to work the land themselves rather than to exploit the local non-Jewish population. Although this was a noble idea, in practical terms it meant that the non-Jewish population was deprived of potential income.

It was only after the Six Day War in 1967 that the socialist aspect of Israeli society began to be eroded—not through a conscious thought process, but by the sudden availability of cheap Palestinian labour. Thus individualism was reinstated too late, and for materialistic rather than idealistic reasons. The first fortunes were made in Israel during this time; capitalism was, for the first time, an attractive alternative to relying on the resources and strength of the collective and all eyes turned toward the United States. Capitalism could not, however, replace or outweigh the positive aspects of socialism. The ultimate result of these developments for Israel is that it has been left in a vacuum, failed both by socialism and capitalism. As long as there were both Communist and capitalist powers in the world that existed in conflict with one another, there was a permanent search for a third way and a natural balance of power. The world seemed to realize that neither capitalism nor Communism provided all the answers. The end of the Cold War, however, brought an imbalance in the global political equilibrium. In the absence of a necessary antipode the United States became the sole superpower.

The last sixty years have made it obvious that Israelis and Palestinians cannot find an acceptable solution on their own and therefore help is needed from the outside. This help cannot come only from one country, however, as has been the case in recent decades with the United States. I always considered it a mistake, or at the very least a great risk, for Israel to lean exclusively on the United States. This dependence changed the very nature of Israeli society to the point that its European heritage was abandoned in favour of a so-called American way of life. Having reached the apex of its powers, the United States has been gradually losing its world hegemony, as has been the case with every superpower in history; in the next twenty or thirty years Israel will have to look for support in Beijing and New Delhi rather than in Washington, and the absence of Jewish communities in these cities will not facilitate the task.

I believe that Israel will also have to invest much more energy in its relations with European countries, above all with Germany. Germany has certainly done everything in its power since the end of the Second World War to help the Jewish people and to demonstrate great sensitivity toward them. I maintain, however, that Germany could be even more helpful by mediating in the Middle East in order to work constructively toward a practicable solution both for Israelis and Palestinians. Intervention of this nature is at present impossible because of the weight of the

Holocaust on the German psyche. Israel could encourage Germany to go beyond the burden of the recent past in order to make a unique contribution to the future of the region, which would in turn be a great gift to Palestinians as well. This, to me, is a logical reflection on the principle of "never again."

There has always been a tendency, in a certain line of Jewish thought, to adhere to the universality of human experience. These thinkers—Spinoza, Heinrich Heine, Martin Buber and Sigmund Freud among others—made no distinction between Jewishness and otherness. The extreme opposite of this broad way of thinking is exemplified by the religious political parties in Israel, who define the occupied territories not only as "liberated" territories, but, even worse, as "biblical, liberated" territories. As I said in my speech at the Hebrew University in Jerusalem in 1996, "The definition of an Orthodox Jew is understood; however, the definition of a secular Jew is complex and until we can make this definition, until we are able to explain what brings a person to be and to feel himself a Jew, we will not be able to explain to ourselves the foundation of our existence; we will also not be able to conduct a dialogue between ourselves, and between ourselves and our Palestinian neighbours." While it remains unclear how, when or even if the conflict will be resolved, it is obvious to me that it will never be achieved by an isolationist or militaristic mentality; the modern definition of Judaism, and of Israel as a Jewish state, must become broader, extrapolating the universalist approach begun by the great Jewish thinkers of the past.

It is essential to understand the difference between power and force, which is related to the distinction between volume and intensity in music: when a musician is told to play with greater intensity, his first reaction is to play louder. In fact, the opposite is required: the lower the volume, the greater the need for intensity; the greater the volume, the less the need for intensity. The effect produced by the huge outpouring of sound in Beethoven or

Wagner is much greater when the sound is not forcefully controlled every step of the way, but rather allowed to grow organically, its natural, inherent power being the result of gradually accumulating strength. The build-up and release of tension are central to the expression of music. Thus even the most powerful chord should be played so that it allows the inner voices to be heard; otherwise it lacks tension and depends exclusively on brutal, aggressive force. One must be able to hear the opposition, the notes that oppose the main idea. In other words the concepts of counterpoint and transparency are ever present in music. If a performance is not aurally transparent, only some of the music is heard, but not the totality. In a perfectly harmonized ensemble in Mozart's operas, every single voice is simultaneously saying something completely different. Despite the varying texts, though, there is a definite sense of organization, sometimes with main and subsidiary voices, sometimes with combinations of both. A Mozart operatic ensemble is never presented exclusively as a simple unit made up of the number of voices in it. It explores all the possible combinations inherent in the number of voices.* Music would be totally uninteresting without this sense of distinct elements. Even at a moment in which they are all unified when everything comes together in a single chord, one must be able to hear all the different voices.

The powerful instruments in the orchestra, such as the trumpets and trombones, must be able to play within the orchestra and not outside it. They must play in such a way that there is a full sense of power while allowing the other instruments, which are less powerful, to be heard at the same time. If they are allowed to overpower the weaker instruments the content of the music will

---

* A quintet, for example, can consist of one unit made up of the five voices, 2+3; 4+1; 2+1+1+1; 2+2+1; or 3+1=1. In each case, the roles can be exchanged during the course of the ensemble piece; the two voices singing together can begin to sing different parts and their unity can be replaced by two other voices.

not be properly understood and the sound will not be powerful, only forced. For this reason, playing in an orchestra requires constant awareness of all the other voices, expressing one's own while at the same time listening to the other. Until Mahler's time, composers marked dynamic changes vertically in the score; in other words, a crescendo is printed in one place and applies to all the instruments in the orchestra. In these cases the conductor and the musicians are left to realize the vertical instruction in a horizontally audible fashion, thus allowing the weaker instruments to begin a crescendo sooner than the brass or the timpani and doing the opposite in a diminuendo. It is possible to mute a trumpet or trombone, but impossible to amplify the flute.

The idea of music, as we see, could be a model for society; it teaches us the importance of the interconnection between transparency, power and force. But if music is so human, so all-inclusive, how is it possible that monsters such as Adolf Hitler had such love for it? How can we explain the fact that Hitler was able to send millions of people to the gas chamber, yet could be moved to tears listening to music? How was Wagner able to compose music of such nobility but also write his despicable anti-Semitic pamphlet, *Das Judentum in der Musik*? I believe there is not enough thought about music, only visceral reactions almost on an animal level. Spinoza believed reason was the saving grace of the human being; we must learn to look at music in the same way as human existence.

The inevitable flow in music means constant movement—development, change, or transformation. Nothing stands still and when it is repeated it is different because of the passage of time. In life, however, the human being not only tends to attempt to dispose of the unpleasurable or the negative as soon as he can but also to hold on as solidly as possible to the pleasurable or the positive. Neither of these desires take into consideration the fact that the human being himself is permanently subject to change and to the speed at which it happens.

The power of music lies in its ability to speak to all aspects of the human being—the animal, the emotional, the intellectual and the spiritual. How often we think that personal, social and political issues are independent, without influencing each other. From music we learn that this is an objective impossibility; there simply are no independent elements. Logical thought and intuitive emotions must be permanently united. Music teaches us, in short, that everything is connected.

Part Two

Variations

1

I Have a Dream

Only twenty-four hours. To change the world you must stick to this timetable. In my dream, I am prime minister of Israel. My baton conducts a magnificent new symphony—a treaty celebrating the harmonious coexistence of Israel and Palestine. In this work I will accomplish what has been impossible until now—the equal rights of these two peoples in the Middle East. The theme of the overture has Jerusalem as the common capital city. This Holy Town should immediately become a shared home for Christians, Muslims and Jews. For me, Jerusalem is a city that still resonates with a history from beyond the ancient civilizations of Rome and Athens.

It is Thursday morning, 8 a.m. A sunny sky, the air mild. It's a pleasant autumn day that has an air about it of history in the making. The philosopher Baruch Spinoza knocks at the door of my residence, diagonally across from the wall of prayers. Though he has been dead for 300 years I have selected him as my adviser. He has brought my favorite food, hummus. There is also fresh pressed orange juice and strong coffee.

Just as we finish strengthening ourselves the phone rings. It is my friend Edward Said. In real life he is Professor of Literature at Columbia University, but in my dream he has been selected by the Palestinians to sign the peace treaty. "Hey," I say to him, "where are you? We want to make peace today and you're going to be late?" When he finally turns up, all three of us know that there will be no turning back. To start with, we decide that the peace treaty will be enacted from May 15: because on this day fifty-one years ago both our peoples were at war. For the Jews it was the War of Independence, for the Palestinians it was *Al Nakba* (the Catastrophe). From tomorrow this anniversary of war will only be known as the "Day of Peace."

Three conditions must be met, or the treaty will not be worth the paper it is written on. First, both nations are obligated to work together. This cooperation will be so tight that not only our economic futures but also our cultural and scientific futures will be interwoven. This ensures that Palestine and Israel will be as close knit as a family. It also implies solidarity. For example, what is to be done with the money European banks stole from the Jews during the Nazi era? My dream is, if there are no survivors to give the money to, Israel should spend the millions of dollars on Palestinian refugees.

Second, I am in favor of arming both nations. Israel must remain vigilant against the Arab world—but so should Palestine (at least for her own peace of mind). It will be very difficult for the ultra-religious Jews to accept this. I'll take options in my treaty to separate church and state—like in the rest of the Western world. I would do everything for the religious and for the study of religion. After all, Judaism is almost a science and the Talmud is much more than just a text we declaim. But what will I do about the specter of radical religious groups . . . ?

Finally, the treaty will provide for the creation of a new domestic secret service, comprising both the army and the police. How about calling it the "Ministry for Peace"? A judge, not a soldier, will lead it. He would ensure a transparency and a conduct that could never last under the hawks of the military. In my dream this would create a new horizon for many. It would be a lively time and emotions might overflow. Whoever strikes out against peace would be sentenced to five years in a kind of gulag. Even Palestinians would be sent here. A type of atonement that will ensure reformed behavior. Let them strike out their own eyes!

Guests begin to arrive as we finish the three pillars of the treaty. Israeli and Palestinian intellectuals, musicians, writers and philosophers. Their opinions are the touchstone for the peace. Cigar smoke hangs in the air. There is much debate. Suddenly there is a knock. The room falls silent and, as one, the heads of my guests turn toward the door. David Ben Gurion has arrived with Gamal Abdel Nasser. In my dream they have formed an alliance and are against my treaty. They direct their contempt at Said and myself, shaking their fingers in the air, chanting words such as "betrayal of Israel" and "betrayal of Arab nationalism."

Unmoved, I explain to them that the time has come to relinquish control over one and a half million Palestinians. We have a duty to move on. It is imperative not only for moral reasons but also for the future of Judaism. If the state of Israel does not learn to embrace peace and open her borders, she risks becoming a ghetto.

It is vital that my people understand that this is not about doing the Palestinians a favor, but rather that this is the one chance we Jews have to evolve. Those who exhaust themselves with war will have no strength left for a future of peace. Ben Gurion and Nasser are impressed.

Then I follow up with a Jewish joke that illustrates the inner struggles of my people. Five Jews meet to decide what is important to the human race. Moses scratches his head and says, "The ability to think." Jesus places hand on heart and says, "Sympathy." Marx rubs his stomach and says, "Food." Freud grabs his crotch and says, "Sex." Einstein touches his knees and says, "Everything is relative." As you see, the joke explains why we Jews are so often consumed by doubt.

The day ends with a celebration. It's time for dinner. The spread is generous: kosher food alongside Arab delicacies. Albert Einstein is there; he is a bit grouchy because he is sure that the gravitational fields between the two camps will rip my plans apart. He sits next to Spinoza who explains how belief in just one view can totally sap one's strength. Naturally, the dramatist Heiner Müller is also present. He smokes a long, distinguished cigar and makes statements such as "Shakespeare uses Hamlet as an alter-ego to change the world." Germany's Chancellor Gerhard Schröder is tolerated because he will donate a case of Cohibas. Ludwig van Beethoven sits at the head of the table, head bowed, sketching notes while dreaming up a fantastic anthem for the two new states. Richard von Weizsacker, good-looking as ever, a great statesman and friend of Israel, speaks of the similarities between Berlin and Jerusalem. I was just thinking whether he should be the first mayor of the new capital Jerusalem, when Martin Luther King Jr. comes through the door. He yells, "You have a dream? It's Barenboim, isn't it?" He grasps me by the shoulders, strokes my hair and says, "I don't know whether to laugh or cry—you're alive and I am dead."

Is this really a dream? In reality, I have already realized my dream on a small scale. This summer I created an orchestra in which young Jewish and Palestinian musicians play together as though they had been doing so for ever. Through music we drove away hostility. It is intolerable to think that as we enter the new millennium, the Middle East shall remain the same as it has been during this century—a powder keg, a region of hatred with peoples in search of national supremacy. In my dream it takes only twenty-four hours to create peace. Politics can take more time, but not endless time.

Original article published in Die Zeit.

2

On Schumann

RONDO *Mr Barenboim, can you imagine returning to your roots some day, perhaps spending all your time at the piano?*
DANIEL BARENBOIM   In essence, I'm already doing that. I have reduced conducting to a minimum. You know, in addition to my home orchestras in Berlin and Chicago, I currently only conduct the Vienna Philharmonic and the Berlin Philharmonic. And I'm once again practicing the piano a great deal. Which, by the way, has become more difficult than in the past. The transition from conducting to playing piano doesn't happen as quickly any more.
RONDO   *You have now been general music director of the Staatsoper Unter den Linden for twelve years. Have you achieved your personal goals, in particular with regard to the sound of the Staatskapelle?*
BARENBOIM   Yes. Oh, yes.
RONDO   *Is the recording of the four Schumann symphonies a milestone for you, or only a way station?*
BARENBOIM   Everything in life is a way station. When I think about Beethoven's Ninth Symphony, which I have been conducting almost every year since 1991, I'm seeing it; I'm hearing it. We actually started down the path with two great cycles as part of our main repertoire—the Wagner operas and the Beethoven symphonies. The Schumann idea came about as a result of a conversation in Vienna, as we presented the

Beethoven cycle there; all of the piano concerti and the symphonies. The director of the music society asked me: "What do you want to do next time? Brahms?" My impression has always been to couple Brahms with, for example, Schoenberg or Schumann, and so we settled on Schumann. That is, a contemporary who did it differently. And, then, we presented the four Schumann and the four Brahms symphonies on four nights in Vienna, as a sort of double cycle, in the combination of one-one, two-two, three-three, four-four.

RONDO   *And what conclusion did you reach after this dissection?*

BARENBOIM   The difference between Schumann and Brahms, personally and orchestrally, is more interesting than what they have in common. Schumann is a very different world.

RONDO   *But what is fundamentally different about Schumann? What makes him unique? And why does the Fourth Symphony, although composed before the Second and Third, segregate itself so clearly from the rest of the framework?*

BARENBOIM   In the Fourth, we sense the spirit of Wagner more clearly than in the other symphonies.

RONDO   *But even in the Third,* Tannhäuser *already shines through, in the fourth movement.*

BARENBOIM   Yes, of course. And Schubert in the first movement. For me, the four symphonies are like an anthology of distinct types. I don't know if one can cloak it in words. Somehow it's clumsy, self-conscious, external to the main idea. Schumann's symphonies are like a human being who doesn't quite fit into society, who thinks differently, who dresses differently. I think what essentially separated Schumann from Brahms is this: he is, far more than Brahms, a composer at the extreme.

RONDO   *Schumann, as it were, throws a curve that always surprises us.*

BARENBOIM   Yes. It's strange, but the orchestration in Schumann's case has often suffered from the fact that the interpreters thought it had to sound like Brahms. But it's a completely different language. What occurs to me is that the more removed we are from a time in history—the more removed we are from a particular epoch—the more we see what the people had in common, and therefore the less that differentiated them. A further problem of the poor reputation of Schumann as a composer of symphonies is that we have not properly read the musical "diary" of this composer, in the case of Schumann that means the piano pieces. A conductor who only views Schumann's symphonies from the orchestral perspective will only understand the works to a limited extent. One needs to think of the symphonies from the point of view of piano pieces, as with Debussy. The associations are significant. Otto Klemperer, for example, believed very strongly in—and agitated himself over—the fact that conductors have no culture and only know what they themselves conduct. Distressingly, this doesn't mean that one can conduct Schumann's symphonies better if one knows his piano pieces well. Nevertheless, one then has a certain head start.

RONDO *Let's deal with the programming of the works. Although Schumann later deleted the appellations to the First and Third Symphonies, that is, "Spring" and "Rheinish," is there a certain poetic intent to be recognized? And does that really mean, in Schumann's case, the program? Can we read it?*

BARENBOIM I don't know. I believe it's unimportant. The problem is that music is not just a collection of tones and sounds. Music aspires to far more, in the sense of what Adorno said about Beethoven's symphonies: that they are a conception of life. The problem appears to me to be that this humanistic idea in music that we now speak of basically can't be expressed in words. If we could do this, the music wouldn't be necessary. Whether you think of spring when you hear the B major Symphony, and I of the desert, is actually not important. The main thing is that this music affects us as humans—emotionally or rationally, in the best case both. How we describe, so to speak, the feelings is less important in the final analysis. It's too bad that today, in our politically correct society, we always expect a message. That is not the correct disposition. Everyone must learn to listen actively. One cannot sit in a chair with a glass of whisky in hand and expect that the music will transport one into another world. The transport has to be ordered, even as it arrives, by us. And there may be conductors who achieve much by attempting to use imagery—I am not one of them. We awaken the associations, the human thoughts, considerably more if we work with musical means and in the process take subtle note of the thoughts. The impressions that one thereby has, do not play the main role. Take, for example, Ravel's *Boléro*. One person sees a single, wonderful, upward assault in it, another experiences the fantasia of repetitiveness, and this opus has even been viewed as a piece of music alluding to coitus.

RONDO   *And the Spring Symphony?*

BARENBOIM   It contains a certain serenity and lightness. For me, the association is with the *Humoresque*, Op. 20 for piano by Schumann. A similar world, a similar rhythm, similar structures are illustrated in it. And the piece is in the same key.

RONDO   *The rhythm in Schumann appears to play a similar, relevant role as with Beethoven. How do you see this?*

BARENBOIM   It isn't the rhythm that plays the decisive role, it's the proper emphasis that's decisive. That is, where the emphasis is not placed. Basically, I believe that too frequently we attempt to solve musical problems in only one direction. In the process, everyone practices the rhythm, the sound, the intonation, the phrasing, the articulation—at least in tonal music one exerts influence on the other. Why is so much spoken today of the selection of the tempo? I do not understand this. As if tempo were an independent phenomenon. The tempo is, however, determined by the content; we don't hear the tempo. We hear only the content. If the tempo is proper for a specific content, then it is correct.

RONDO *But then there would still be the problem of the sensed and the real time.*

BARENBOIM In this regard, I will tell you a story. As a young man, Sergiu Celibidache heard Furtwängler's interpretation of Beethoven's Fifth every night and, every night, it was different, in particular as far as the tempo was concerned. Thereupon, Celibidache asked, "Herr Doktor Furtwängler, how do you determine the tempo?" Furtwängler responded: "Depending on how it sounds." It took years until I understood the deep, philosophical significance of this remark. I believe that musicians come to terms with tempo far too soon. One must, however, also establish the sound content to a much greater extent. The decision on tempo is last. Only at the moment when I comprehend the piece, the content, the sound—consequently everything that belongs to it—do I ask the question, "What tempo suits this?"

RONDO *Schumann himself in later years corrected the metronome information for his symphony. Did he get a different feel for the timing?*

BARENBOIM No. He heard the pieces. Why is so much metronome data by composers too rapid? Because the composer does not physically hear the piece. When they write it they only hear it in their heads. The weight of the sound isn't present. Imagine a poem that you learn by heart. You read it much slower than you remember it in your head. Another example: As I was about to play number VII, the *Notation* of Pierre Boulez, for the first time, I found the tempo indication "quarter note = 60" in the score. To me, it appeared too rapid, I conducted the work at "eighth note = 90"—and Boulez was satisfied. When I asked him how that was possible—after all, he was not only a renowned composer but also an experienced conductor—he said, "When I compose I cook with water, when I conduct I cook with fire." Very French. But correct. I think that's the point. One speaks of the sound as if it were only color. But the weight of the sound is not subjective, but rather objective. And therefore, metronome data is frequently too rapid. For all that, what one must respect is the relationship of the tempos to one another.

RONDO   *Isn't this exactly what's more difficult with Schumann, due to the fitful nature of the course of the music?*

BARENBOIM   Absolutely.

RONDO   *In the Fourth Symphony, it appears to me that your interpretation is a bit too drawn-out, too emphatic. Is a conscious attempt concealed behind this—that is, with a view to Schumann, who once called the work a "symphonic fantasy"?*

BARENBOIM   Yes. The feel of the tempo in the first movement is completely different from that of the other symphonies, maybe that is the reason. But listen to the Fourth with Furtwängler. For Furtwängler, it is not important whether it is slower or more rapid, whether the tempo changes itself organically or not. What is important, and what places Furtwängler above the rest for me, is that the musical discourse is influenced, imprinted by the harmonic tension as with no other conductor. I will give you an example: if, in Beethoven's Fourth Symphony, immediately after the exposition, there is a sudden transition into a totally alien key, according to B major, you almost need a visa to go there, this key is so alien. Furtwängler accomplished the transition like no other. And why? Because he was able to make the new harmonic realization clear. To come back to Schumann's Fourth, I believe the work moves at a very different speed harmonically. The harmonic tensions are different, despite the chromaticism in the other symphonies. And that is at least as important. In the Fourth, the vertical pressure is much greater. One cannot express this with any other sound. If one wants to experience the "Es" [E flat] as a shock in the course of execution for ears that are used to living in D minor, it takes time. The tonality has to be established.

RONDO *Does the selection of the key play a leading role in Romanticism? Does it describe a certain state of being, as was the case with Beethoven? If Salopp were asked: Would the same tension be possible if the Fourth were in A minor?*

BARENBOIM I don't know. Kubelik contends certain keys are the same as certain colors. In A minor, the piece must first be instrumentally different. You know, I grew up with a completely different relationship to keys. I studied harmonics and composition under Nadia Boulanger. I was twelve years old when I had my first hour with her. She was an older lady and appeared, to me at that time, like a museum piece. She introduced me to the Prelude and Fugue in Es [E flat]-minor from volume one of the *Well-Tempered Clavier* and said, "Now, young man, you will play that in A minor."

RONDO *Could you?*

BARENBOIM The prelude was OK. But the five-voice fugue was hardly doable ad hoc. But Boulanger trained me that way: every week, a prelude and fugue. This forced me to realize the harmonic relationship independent of a specific key. I am, therefore, the wrong person to ask about transcribability.

RONDO *Then perhaps this one. In 1841, as Schumann first spied the light of the world in Leipzig, fifty musicians—violins and even violas—played in the Gewandhaus Orchestra. Purists contend that the circumstances of this performance would have to be re-created in order to play an authentic Schumann. What do you think about that?*

BARENBOIM Mozart was highly impressed when, in Mannheim, he had twenty first violins for a performance of his C major Symphony, No. 34. What do the purists think of that?

RONDO *A recommendation for compromise: would it be possible with fifty musicians?*

BARENBOIM Naturally. It depends on the space. In the Palais Lobkovitz, where Eroica was first played, one can of course play with six first violins. The most important thing, be it easy or difficult, slow or fast, in the final analysis is: does the content come through? Is the relationship between vertical pressure and horizontal discourse correct? Just as in our lives. We speak about music as if it were an island that lay aside the world. This is wrong. If I want to have contact with anyone, the important thing for me is how he lives the moments, the most important, almost historical moments. The main issue is how one can experience these tensions and relaxations within the harmonic world, at what intensity and speed. And can I put the music to it such that, when I come to the last note, I can re-experience it in its entirety. This influences my musical thinking more than anything else.

RONDO   *Apropos influence: is Furtwängler the role model for Schumann?*

BARENBOIM   He is a role model for everything. That does not mean that I imitate him. If I try to understand why he has done a certain thing, then I am on the right path. But I use my own means. In that regard, he is my role model for everything. You can learn a lot more from him than from all the other conductors.

Interview with Juergen Otten for Rondo *magazine, January 2004*

3

Remembering Edward Said

SEPTEMBER 25, 2003

Perhaps the first thing one remembers about Edward Said was his breadth of interest. He was not only at home in music, literature, philosophy, or the understanding of politics, but also he was one of those rare people who saw the connections and the parallels between different disciplines, because he had an unusual understanding of the human spirit, and of the human being, and he recognized that parallels and paradoxes are not contradictions.

He saw in music not just a combination of sounds, but he understood the fact that every musical masterpiece is, as it were, a conception of the world. And the difficulty lies in the fact that this conception of the world cannot be described in words—because were it possible to describe it in words, the music would be unnecessary. But he recognized that the fact that it is indescribable doesn't mean it has no meaning.

This very curious mind, of course, allowed him privileged glimpses into the subconscious of people, of creators. And added to that he had a very unrestrained courage of utterance, and this is what earned him the admiration, the jealousy and the enmity of so many people.

Many Israelis and Jews did not want to tolerate his criticism, not just of the present Israeli government, but of a certain mentality that he identified in Israeli thoughts and deeds—namely the lack of empathy with the fact that the very same War of

Independence of Israel in 1948, which brought about the acquisition of a new identity for the Jewish part of the population, was not just a military defeat but also a psychological catastrophe for the non-Jewish population of Palestine. And therefore he was critical of the inability of Israeli leaders to make the necessary symbolic gestures that have to precede any political solution. The Arabs, on the other hand, were and are still unable to accept his sensitivity toward Jewish history, limiting themselves to repeat their innocence as far as the suffering of Jewish people is concerned.

It was precisely this ability of his to see not only the different aspects of any thought or process but also their inevitable consequences as well—and also the combination of human, psychological and historical, as the case may be, "pre-history" of such thoughts and processes. He was one of those rare people who was permanently aware of the fact that information is only the very first step toward understanding. And he always looked for the "beyond" in the idea, the "unseen" by the eye, the "unheard" by the ear.

It was a combination of all these qualities that led him to found together with me the West-Eastern Divan, which provides a forum for young Israeli and Arab musicians to learn together music and all its ramifications.

The Palestinians have lost one of the most eloquent defenders of their aspirations. The Israelis have lost an adversary—but a fair and humane one. And I have lost a soul mate.

SEPTEMBER 2004

Edward Said was many things for many people, but in reality his was a musician's soul, in the deepest sense of the word.

He wrote about important universal issues such as exile, politics, integration. However, the most surprising thing for me, as his friend and great admirer, was the realization that, on many occasions, he actually formulated ideas and reached conclusions through music; and, along the same lines, he saw music as a reflection of the ideas that he had regarding other issues. This is one of the main reasons why I believe that Said was an extremely important figure. His journey through this world took place precisely at a time when the humanity of music, its human value as well as the value of thought, the transcendence of the idea written in sounds, were, and regrettably continue to be, concepts in decline.

His fierce antispecialization led him to criticize very strongly, and in my opinion very fairly, the fact that musical education was becoming increasingly poor, not only in the United States—which, after all, had imported the music of the Old Europe—but also in the very countries that had produced music's greatest figures: for example, in Germany, which had produced Beethoven, Brahms, Wagner, Schumann and many others, or in France, which had produced Debussy and Ravel. In all these countries, which had been the cradle of musical creation, musical education was in rapid decline. Furthermore, he perceived a sign that bothered him exceedingly, a perception that was to unite us very quickly: even when there was musical education, it was carried out in a very specialized way. In the best of cases, young people were offered the opportunity to practice an instrument, to acquire inevitably necessary knowledge of theory, of musicology and of everything that a musician needs professionally. But, at the same time, there existed a widespread and growing incomprehension of a simultaneously simple and complex problem: that is, the impossibility of articulating with words the content of a musical work. After all, if it were possible to express in words the content of one of Beethoven's symphonies, we would no longer have a need for that symphony. But the fact that it is impossible to express in words the music's content does not mean that there is no content. That is why I assert that the question is simultaneously simple and complex.

This is a tendency that leads to an impoverished and narrow specialization. In the case of outstanding talents, this results in mechanization of the instrument, and in the case of creation it leads composers to an incapacity to express that very richness that the human being discovered the potential to express through sound.

The paradox consists in the fact that music is only sound, but sound, in itself, is not music. There lies Said's main idea as a musician who—on a biographical note—was also an excellent pianist. In recent years, due to his terrible illness, he was unable to maintain the level of physical energy necessary to play the piano. I remember many unforgettable times that we spent playing Schubert pieces for four hands.

Two or three years ago, I had a concert at Carnegie Hall in New York and he was going through a very difficult period of his illness. The concert was on a Sunday afternoon. Although he knew that I had arrived that very morning from Chicago, he showed up very early at rehearsal with a volume of Schubert's pieces for four hands. He told me: "Today I want us to play at least eight bars, not for the pleasure of playing, but because I need it to survive." As it is easy to imagine, at that moment, just in from the airport and with one hour of rehearsal before the afternoon's concert, what he was proposing to me was the last thing that could have interested me. But, as is always the case in life, when you teach, you learn, and when you give, you receive. And you learn when you teach because the student asks questions which you no longer even ask yourself, because they are part of the almost automatic thought that each one of us develops. And suddenly the question addresses something that forces us to rethink it from its origin, from its very essence. That is why, in the same way, when you give you receive, because it is when you least expect it. To receive something when one expects to receive it is much less interesting. Why do I say this? Because I was there, and really, the last thing I wanted to do was to play Schubert for four hands. Naturally, I did it, with the greatest pleasure, because my dear friend, whom I so admired and loved, asked me to do so. But when we played, with him, those few minutes of a Schubert rondo—an extremely beautiful piece, which was not, however, the deepest or most transcendent—I felt musically enriched in a completely unexpected way. That was Edward Said.

Said was interested in detail. Indeed, he understood perfectly that musical genius or musical talent requires tremendous attention to detail. The genius attends to detail as though it were the most important thing. And in doing so he does not lose sight of the big picture; rather, he manages to trace out that big picture. Because the big picture, in music as in thought, must be the result of the coordination of small details. For that reason, when he listened to or spoke of music, he focused his attention on the small details that many professionals have not even discovered.

He had a refined knowledge of the art of composition and orchestration. He knew that in the second act of *Tristan und Isolde*, at a certain moment the horns withdraw behind the stage and, a couple bars later, the same musical note re-emerges in the pit orchestra's clarinets. What a number of singers I have had the honor and pleasure of collaborating with on that piece, who are unaware of that detail and look behind them to see where the sound is coming from! They don't know that the note is no longer coming from behind the stage, but rather from the pit. He took interest in these things and was concerned with the detail itself, the value of the whole notwithstanding, because he understood that this meticulous interest in detail conferred upon the whole a grandeur that it cannot acquire without this profound concern for detail.

He also knew how to distinguish clearly between power and force, which constituted one of the main ideas of his struggle. He knew quite well that, in music, force is not power, something which many of the world's political leaders do not perceive. The difference between power and force is equivalent to the difference between volume and intensity in music. When one speaks with a musician and says to him, "You are not playing intensely enough," his first reaction is to play louder. And it is exactly the opposite: the lower the volume, the greater the need for intensity, and the greater the volume, the greater the need for a calm force in the sound.

These are some examples that illustrate my conviction that his concept of life and of the world originated and lay in music. Another example is to be found in his idea of interconnection. In music, there are no independent elements. How often we think, on a personal, social, or political level, that there are certain independent things and that, upon doing them, they will not influence others or that this interconnection will remain hidden. This does not occur in music, because in music everything is interconnected. The character and intention of the simplest melody change drastically with a complex harmony. That is learned through music, not through political life. Thus emerges the impossibility of separating elements, the perception that everything is connected, the need always to unite logical thought and intuitive emotion. How often all of us think that we should consider something objectively. We know all too well, but we forget, that emotion will not allow us to do so. How often do we succumb to the temptation of abandoning all logic for the sake of an emotional need, an emotional whim, for the seduction of emotion? In music this is impossible, since music cannot be made exclusively with reason or with emotion. What is more: if those elements may be separated, they are no longer music, but a collection of sounds. If the listener, upon hearing something, can affirm that "it has an impressive logic, but emotionally it wasn't convincing"; or, in contrast, "how appealing I found it, what an exciting emotive force it has, though it wasn't very logical"; for me, this is no longer music. It wasn't for Said, either.

His concept of inclusion as opposed to exclusion also derived from music, as well as the integration principle, applicable to all sorts of problems. The same could be applied to the discussion of his book *Orientalism*. It speaks of the idea of Oriental seduction versus Western production. In music, there is no production without seduction. There is seduction without production, but not production without seduction. Productive as a musical idea may be, if it is lacking the seduction of the necessary sound, it is insufficient. This is why I say that Edward Said was, for many, a great thinker, a fighter for the rights of his people and an incomparable intellectual. But for me he was always, really, a musician in the deepest sense of the term.

For me, personally, the loss of Edward Said has been a terrible blow, because it affects me in so many different areas. His friendship represented an intellectual stimulation such as I have never had and which I will surely never have again, a deep friendship such as I have only rarely experienced, the possibility to share so many serious and banal pleasures and, not so much as gastronomy, smoking cigars. In so many different ways, since the loss of Said, I feel much poorer than I would like to feel and imagine.

The Palestinian people lost, with his death, one of their most lucid advocates, although he was and is very criticized in his own country. For Israel he was a formidable adversary, although he called for mutual recognition and acceptance of the other's suffering. Yet how many Israeli leaders would have wanted to forget the existence of Edward Said!

Translated from the Spanish by Kimberly Borchard.

.

4

I Was Reared on Bach

NOVEMBER 2004

I was reared on Bach. My father was virtually my only teacher, and he attached great importance to my growing up with Bach's keyboard music. He considered it to be very important, not only for its musical and pianistic aspects, but also for everything else that is played on the piano. For him polyphonic music making was simply one of the most important issues concerning everything relating to piano playing. In itself the piano cannot seduce by virtue of its sound alone. The listener can be seduced by the lovely sound of, for example, a violin or an oboe. The piano, on the other hand, is a neutral instrument, and the art of playing it involves a sleight of hand. It is possible to create the illusion of a legato on the piano although, in the physical sense, it is impossible. But it is possible to create the illusion of sustained sound similar to that of a string instrument. The most important part of piano playing is the symphonic element. The music can only be of interest if the different strands of the polyphonic texture are played so distinctly that they can all be heard and create a three-dimensional effect—just as in painting, where something is moved into the foreground and something else into the background, making one appear closer to the viewer than the other, although the painting is one-dimensional.

In my childhood I played practically all the preludes and fugues from *The Well-Tempered Clavier* and many other pieces by Bach.

That was my basis. At the age of twelve I moved to Paris to study harmony and counterpoint with Nadia Boulanger. When I arrived for my first lesson, *The Well-Tempered Clavier* was on the music stand of the grand piano. She turned the pages forward and back; finally she settled on the Prelude in E minor from Book One and said: "Right, my boy, now play it for me in A minor." She held a wooden ruler in her hand and every time my fingers played a wrong note she tapped them with it. Thus *The Well-Tempered Clavier* became the foundation for everything.

In addition my father communicated something to me that I only found expressed in words when I was an adult—in a book about Franz Liszt in Weimar. It describes how he explained to a pupil that the piano should not be played with two hands or as two units. Either you play with a unit consisting of two hands, or with ten units in which each finger is independent. This is a very important piece of advice. I was really pleased to read that, because I recognized once again what my father had taught me without putting it into words. This is the only way to tackle Bach. One might well imagine a nocturne by Chopin with the melody in the right hand and the accompaniment in the left, without any polyphony. But Bach's keyboard works definitely call for ten fingers that are independent of one another. And if they are, they can be brought together to create a unit.

One element in tonal music that is frequently neglected these days is harmony. Harmonic tensions have a crucial effect on a work and the way in which it is played. Of the three elements—harmony, rhythm and melody—which have such a profound influence on tonal music, harmony is perhaps the most important, because it is the most potent. You can play the same chord with millions of different rhythms. It can cope with them all without needing to change. A melody is uninteresting if it does not move harmonically. That implies that the impact of harmony is much greater than that of rhythm and melody.—And it exists in every tonal work. There are thousands of distinctions between Bach, Wagner, Tchaikovsky and Debussy, but they have one thing in common: harmonic impact. This implies that a chord exerts a kind of vertical pressure on the horizontal movement of the music. When a chord moves, the horizontal flow of the music is changed. This has nothing to do with Bach or Chopin or anyone else; in my opinion it is a law of nature.

The study of old instruments and historic performance practice has taught us a great deal, but the main point, the impact of harmony, has been ignored. This is proved by the fact that tempo is described as an independent phenomenon. It is claimed that one of Bach's gavottes must be played fast and another slowly. But tempo is not independent. And you do not hear it. You only hear the substance of the music. It is this very audibility that informs every kind of musical theory. I could develop a theory that applies to any phrase of any prelude or fugue by Bach. But all theory is useless if it cannot be heard when you play. I think that concerning oneself purely with historic performance practice and the attempt to reproduce the sound of older styles of music making is limiting and no indication of progress. Mendelssohn and Schumann tried to introduce Bach into their own period, as did Liszt with his transcriptions and Busoni with his arrangements. In America Leopold Stokowski also tried to do it with his arrangements for orchestra. This was always the result of "progressive" efforts to bring Bach closer to the particular period. I have no philosophical problem with someone playing Bach and making it sound like Boulez. My problem is more with someone who tries to imitate the sound of that time. Knowing that in Bach's day this appoggiatura was played slowly and that ornamentation fast, and copying it is not enough. I must understand why it was like that. This is why I consider a purely academic approach to the past very dangerous because it is linked to ideology and fundamentalism, even in music. Today we are witnesses to the suffering and violence that are the product of fundamentalism.

In Bach's works there is a powerful bond between rhythm and harmony. There is a symbiotic relationship between these two elements, which is probably unique among composers. Maybe this is what one might term the epic quality in Bach, just as there is a dramatic quality in Haydn, Mozart and Beethoven. Thanks to this epic quality, everything in Bach's music achieves unity. An excellent example is the C sharp fugue from Book One of *The Well-Tempered Clavier*. It is like a dance with enormous rhythmic vitality. Any knowledge acquired when dealing with harmony is immensely helpful. Now, when I delve more deeply into or play *The Well-Tempered Clavier*, I often remember many musical experiences—with Mozart, Wagner, Schoenberg and many others—and observe that the greater the general knowledge of music, the more interesting the performance.

Why did Bülow describe *The Well-Tempered Clavier* as the Old Testament? What is the Old Testament? On the one hand it is the narrative of a people and its experiences. On the other, it is a compilation of thoughts about life on this earth, love, ethics, morals and human qualities. Thoughts on the experience of the past provide a statement about the present and also a lesson for the future, showing thoughtful people where and how they can find their own way. That is what the Old Testament means to me, as does every other masterpiece, including *The Well-Tempered Clavier*. It makes a statement about everything that preceded it in music. It makes a statement about music in the time of Bach. But it also indicates the direction music might take as it develops—as indeed it has developed. For example, the chromaticism in the Prelude in C sharp minor from Book One brings Wagner's *Tristan und Isolde* to mind. Or the Fugue in E flat, which could be straight out of a symphony by Bruckner. In other words, *The Well-Tempered Clavier* is not only the sum of everything that has preceded it, but it also points the way ahead. In the history of European music there are very few composers whose works that applies. This is one of the main reasons for the towering stature of Bach's music.

Recorded by Axel Brüggemann for Der Tagesspiegel *translated by Gery Bramall.*

5

On Wilhelm Furtwängler

NOVEMBER 2004

Wilhelm Furtwängler was always a stranger in this world. He was someone who went his own way and stood apart from the others: he could not be pigeonholed in any one category, no matter how broad. Furtwängler is the ultimate embodiment of the musician who refuses to adapt to pre-existing molds, the anti-ideologue par excellence—and I mean the present tense here quite seriously, for this is what makes Furtwängler still so vivid for us today. On the one hand as musical director of the Berlin Philharmonic he belonged to the establishment, but at the same time in musical terms he was considered an outsider from the very beginning. Contemporaries like Toscanini and Bruno Walter, for example, toed the line much more closely in aesthetic terms. It might seem bizarrely ironic to us today, but in fact the émigré conductors were much less torn figures than Furtwängler, who did not leave Nazi Germany.

The fissures in Furtwängler were internal ones. He was a subjectivist who philosophized. And this is exactly what he expresses in his work: the philosopher led the rehearsal, while the poet conducted in the evening. The one could not have existed without the other. Sharp tongues might claim that this indecision, this ambiguity, was his fate. I don't believe that. Furtwängler was convinced that everything is connected: music as an organic whole. For Furtwängler there were no phenomena independent of one another.

How, we might ask, was he then able to survive intellectually
and politically through the Third Reich?
Of course, as I child I knew who Furtwängler was. I had heard
him in Buenos Aires conducting the *St. Matthew Passion* and
naturally it was something very special when I was introduced
to him in the summer of 1954. Just think: I loved to play the piano; I
would have played for anybody, even the hotel waiter. But this man
had a great aura about him. Today, I can imagine that Furtwängler
must have been very insecure as a person, very vulnerable. And
also very German. Furtwängler needed his musical home. Perhaps
that's why he never accepted the end of tonality.
It's constantly being said that Furtwängler was conservative.
But that's not true, especially when it comes to the young
Furtwängler, who conducted Stravinsky's *Sacre* and later Schoenberg's Variations for Orchestra. Furtwängler had a deep-seated
belief that music must evolve. Music is sound and sound has to
become, not just "be." As a result of this understanding, his music
was always new and never just a question of the repertoire.
Furtwängler did not rehearse just in order to call up what he
discovered in rehearsal for a concert in the evening. For Furtwängler, a Beethoven symphony was just as new, just as vital, as a
piece composed yesterday.
Despite all his distance from the world, all his wanting to be
divorced from the present time and the technological innovations
of his day, he flew in drafty propeller planes to South America
whenever a lucrative offering attracted him there and already his
work in the early 1920s we would consider "jet-setting" today.
When he took over the direction of the Berlin Philharmonic in
1922, he was also active at Leipzig's Gewandhaus and in Vienna.
Looking back at the programs of these years leads us to draw but
one conclusion: the man must have spent most of his time living
on night trains.

Original article published in Der Tagesspiegel.

6

On Pierre Boulez

How Pierre Boulez and I first came to make music together is a rather long story. I had been invited to play with the Berlin Philharmonic by Wilhelm Furtwängler in 1954, when I was eleven years old. My father declined the invitation, telling Furtwängler that he felt that this was the greatest honor that he could bestow upon me, but that we were a Jewish family that had immigrated to Israel only one and a half years earlier and that he, my father, felt it was too soon—a mere nine years after the end of the war—for our family to go to Germany, which Furtwängler understood and accepted very simply and genuinely. And Furtwängler proceeded to write a letter that opened many doors for me in the 1950s in Europe and, I must say also, in America.

Nine years after that, in 1963, I finally decided to go to Germany and played my first concert in Berlin with the radio orchestra for the American sector, the RIAS Symphony Orchestra, as it was then called. After the concert I had a visit from Wolfgang Stresemann, who was the general manager of the Berlin Philharmonic at the time, and who was the son of Germany's last foreign minister before Hitler, a great personality. He was very complimentary about my playing of Beethoven's Fifth Piano Concerto and said that he knew that Furtwängler had invited me to play with the Berlin Philharmonic; now that I had decided to come to Germany, would I agree to play with the orchestra? So I said, yes, of course I would be very happy and honoured to do that. This was late in the season—I think it was in April or May of 1963—and he said that all the programs for the next season were already completed. There was only one where the soloist was not yet announced, and this was in a series of music of the twentieth century; a young French composer who had started conducting a few years earlier by the name of Pierre Boulez was to conduct the concert and would like to do the Bartók First Piano Concerto in the second half of the program. If I wanted to play that, it would be wonderful. And I replied, I don't know the Bartók First Piano Concerto; I have never heard it; I have never seen the music; does it have to be that piece? And he said, if you want to play next season, it has to be this work because it's the only program left—this will be the first season in the new concert hall, the Philharmonie, which they have just finished building, and all the programs are done. I asked for a few days to get the music and look at it. I got the music and I must say, I fell in love with the piece, although it seemed to me then and seems all the more so now, devilishly difficult. But I thought, yes, yes, and I agreed. I have to admit I had not heard the name Pierre Boulez, which is no reflection on him but rather on my ignorance. But I was very, very happy and worked very hard, and learned the piece.

A year later, in the spring of 1964, I played Bartók's First Concerto for the first time with Pierre Boulez. It was an unforgettable experience on many accounts, first of all because I was absolutely fascinated by his musical personality and his way of looking at music in different ways, but also because it was a very difficult program. It had his *Livre pour cordes*, Schoenberg's *Music for a film scene*, and Debussy's *Jeux*, I think—all works which the orchestra did not know—and then the Bartók concerto, which had not been played there since 1926. And this was 1964! So it was a very difficult program. Our rehearsal period was sparse, and I'm sure Pierre Boulez used his time very economically, but, if I may venture to say so, I think he might have underestimated the difficulty of the Bartók First Piano Concerto, especially in those days. It was not a repertoire piece. Géza Anda used to play it, but almost nobody else.

In any event, there was not enough rehearsal time. And so the experience was unforgettable, as I said, on many accounts, one of them being that I felt for the twenty-three minutes that it takes to play the concerto that I was on the most slippery, uncontrollable ground for what seemed to me like twenty-four hours, not a few minutes. Anyway, we got through it and he must have been pleased with me, because very soon after that I had an invitation to play with him in what I think was the first performance in France of the Berg *Kammerkonzert* and Schoenberg piano pieces, in a series he directed in Paris at the time called Le Domaine Musical—concerts of chamber music, mostly dedicated to the music of the day.

And that was the beginning of a very close musical collaboration, and also of a very close and to me very important personal and artistic friendship with him for over forty years. When I became music director of the Orchestre de Paris in 1974, he had already left Paris to protest against many things over which he disagreed with the culture ministry at the time. And he then convinced the President of France, Georges Pompidou, to build IRCAM, the centre for music/acoustic research and coordination in Paris. And in this way Pompidou persuaded him to come back to Paris and Boulez lifted, if you want, a ban that he had imposed that the Orchestre de Paris depended on the Ministry of Culture.

Boulez came and conducted in my very first season in Paris. I must say it was one of the most wonderful things one could imagine to have Pierre Boulez on the scene—he conducted not only when he was invited to conduct, but often he very kindly jumped in when there were cancellations. It was a great luxury, and we shared many of our views about music and especially

about the role of contemporary music. So it was heart-warming
and a source of great artistic support to me. And therefore when I
came to Chicago as music director, he was the first person I
invited as a guest conductor, and relations between him and the
musicians of the orchestra was so good and so fruitful that I asked
him whether he would become principal guest conductor. The rest
is history.

I was born in Argentina and moved to Israel when I was ten;
these were my formative years. For me, contemporary music at
the time was the music of Bartók, who had died seven years before
we moved to Israel, and Stravinsky, who was still alive and whom
I later met. And I knew the Soviet composers, especially those
who wrote for piano—Prokofiev and Shostakovich—and the
lesser composers, Kabalevsky and Khachaturian. But the names of
the major composers who were important were Bartók, Stravinsky, Shostakovich and Prokofiev. On my first concert in New
York I played the first Prokofiev concerto and also played the first
performance outside the Soviet Union of Prokofiev's Ninth
Sonata, soon after his death in the beginning of 1955. But
somehow it didn't really satisfy me completely. And although
I didn't know Bartók's First Piano Concerto, I played the Suite
Op. 14 and other piano pieces. And Stravinsky, of course, the
sonata. I had studied conducting in Salzburg with Igor Marke-
vitch, who was perhaps the strongest champion of *The Rite of
Spring* in those days.

But when Boulez came and we prepared and performed
Berg's *Kammerkonzert*, it was the first time I came in contact
with the Second Viennese School, which was a major hole in
my education. And it was remarkable to see somebody who
understood so well the stretching of the possibilities of harmony
in Schoenberg's early years, and then his eventual break from
it, and the development of the twelve-tone system. It was very
important to encounter someone who came to music much less
from the harmonic basis, as I had done, and who saw music

from the point of view of the structure of the phrases and the form of the pieces.

In any case Boulez the conductor not only made the music of the Second Viennese School more accessible, but made it an integral part of the regular repertoire of the orchestras. He had an ability to render this music so much more transparently than the public was used to, thereby making it possible to discover the many layers of musical structure and subtleties—leading the way for many musicians to approach this music with a degree of understanding that would have been totally impossible without the audibility of its details. If one has to point to his central contribution as a conductor, it must be his ability to make every single note audible in even the most complex scores. All the lines are audible and that is the prerequisite for his followers each to attempt to read between the lines in his own individual way.

I came to his music later. The first piece I studied was *Le marteau sans maître*. And the first work of his that I conducted was a movement out of *Pli selon pli*, if I'm not mistaken, which had a singer in it, but he made an orchestral version without the singer so that I could take the piece on tour to the Soviet Union. With the Orchestre de Paris I then conducted *Rituel* and other pieces, and later commissioned *Notations*, which was to be twelve pieces for orchestra. Four of those were delivered in 1979 and we premiered them in 1980. And I had the good fortune to conduct those four *Notations* with many different orchestras, and very consistently through these twenty-five years. I have seen his pieces become part of my repertoire and also part of the regular repertoire of orchestras. Which brings me to one of the most important points about contemporary music on which he and I agree wholeheartedly, and that is that the problem with contemporary music very often is that the works are not repeated often enough. As a result it isn't possible to get the necessary familiarity—first of all, for the orchestra. By playing a new piece once and preparing it very well and never doing it again, the orchestra cannot achieve the familiarity that it requires to play the piece with enough freedom. And, of course, for the public as well. I think it was Nietzsche who said that in the end we only like what we already know, or what reminds us of something we already know. And that's of course very true; in other words familiarity does not have to breed only contempt.

I've seen this happen with *Notations*, which have become part of the regular repertoire of the Orchestre de Paris. And I have seen these four *Notations* become a regular part of the Staatskapelle repertoire in Berlin, which had no previous association with this type of music. I've done it several times with the Berlin Philharmonic and in Chicago, of course, it is now a completely natural part of the repertoire.

Boulez's works always manage to give you the maximum possibilities with the material involved. In other words, if he has a choice between writing something very simply or making it more complex but more colorful and more interesting, of course he would choose the latter. He is not of the school that believes that the last stroke a composer has to put on his music is the stroke that brings the work to its utmost simplicity. I don't think he even thinks of that; it's of no interest to him whatsoever. What is of greater concern to him is how to make these materials as interesting as possible, and if it means making them more complex he will do so. He also has, of course, the most imaginative sense of orchestration, so that when you get to the orchestral pieces like *Notations*, even people who have difficulty relating to the musical idiom are struck by the multitude of orchestral colors. The aspect of color orchestration is an integral part of his musical ideas. I'm sure he imagines the material in an abstract way as a row of notes, but immediately thereafter, I suspect—and this is pure speculation on my part—he immediately attaches some kind of orchestral color to it. It's not something that is put on as the whipped cream on the cake. It's part of the cake.

To understand Boulez's well-known rebellion against his

upbringing and against French musical culture, it is important to understand French musical life, which, as far as the repertoire is concerned, is a totally illogical sequence of events. When you think that *The Rite of Spring* was performed in Paris before the Brahms D minor Piano Concerto, you realise that something is wrong. *The Rite of Spring* was premiered in Paris in 1913; the Brahms concerto was first performed in Paris in 1936 by Artur Schnabel. So when one says that Pierre Boulez was critical of French musical life, he was critical of it in so many ways because there was a lot to criticize. There were so many important musical developments missing in France, added to which there was a very limited chauvinistic view of all French music, regardless of its quality. Pierre Boulez was always an internationalist, with the capacity to see individual national contributions as elements leading to further developments of the art and the science of music.

Pierre Boulez's rebellions throughout his life were so strong and so successful because he had knowledge of all the above. He knew a lot of the music of the past, and he didn't see the music of his day as a break from the past but as an inevitable follow-up. This was also a new way of thinking, because the traditionalists saw the world of tonal music as basically coming to an end with *Tristan*; after that there was a complete break and then the beginning of something new—atonality. But instead of that, Boulez made the connection. And this is why his advocacy of Mahler, for example, must be seen in that light, in the sense of evolution. In other words Boulez was a revolutionary, but a revolutionary for evolution, not simply for the sake of revolution. I think this is the most extraordinary thing about him—he was not just saying that the past was over and that we have to start something different now.

He was also one of the first musicians who understood the French music of the early part of the twentieth century, primarily Debussy and Ravel—and especially Debussy, I must say—as something more than just color. It has depth, articulation. He found the real richness of Debussy's idiom in so many different ways. Some composers are fortunate in that they have inspired a history of performance from many angles. Debussy, to this day, has had very few advocates, and at the beginning the greatest advocate of his music on the piano was Walter Gieseking, who played it really very beautifully, but in a completely one-dimensional way. Everything is ethereal; everything is a wash of color. And suddenly came Pierre Boulez with such a sense of structure. And he gave not only wonderful performances of Debussy's music, but he gave a very clear direction toward understanding the depth of this music.

I remember Boulez coming to a concert of Bruckner's Eighth, which I conducted in Paris, and he said oh, this music is so simplistic. And I said, but the slow movement should provide interest for you with rhythms that go two against three. Oh, he said, that was done much earlier and much better by Wagner in the second act of *Tristan*. With that sentence he finished off Bruckner. But I must say that ten years or so later, he showed his greatness and intelligence by assimilating a lot of things that he might not have seen before, which is a wonderful lesson for us, because often there are people who have very clear ideas and causes to fight for, and they hold on to them and are immovable. And that is very courageous and very laudable, actually. But there's one step even higher than that, and this is what Boulez represents to me. He knows that certain decisions or opinions that he arrives at are linked to a certain age and to a certain time. In the 1970s it was practically necessary for him *not* to see the beauties in Bruckner, because he was fighting causes that were to him much more important, and rightly so.

And those causes not only demanded his time, but his mind demanded his concentration on them, which were musically from a totally different planet than Bruckner. But after he went through that stage, he could have an open mind for the beauties of this other type of music. Although Pierre Boulez is a man full of seeming contradictions and paradoxes, in fact he is not. There's nothing contradictory about his opinions or about his actions, but rather he has a sense of the necessary clarity of thought that he needs at a given moment. When that moment is over, he is willing and able to examine those thoughts at another time and in another context, and this is a very rare quality.

An edited version appeared in the Chicago Sunday Times.

7

On Don Giovanni

DECEMBER 2007

The Italian term *dramma giocoso*—literally, playful drama— which Mozart applied to the opera *Don Giovanni*, is at once a contradiction in terms and a definition of the very essence not only of this piece but of music itself. Even the funeral march of Beethoven's Eroica Symphony on the one hand, or a waltz by Johann Strauss on the other, inevitably contains an element of its emotional counterpart. The simple act of producing sound is a life-affirming act, which both deepens and relieves the sense of tragedy in the funeral march. Conversely, the Strauss waltz that may be perceived as pleasant and entertaining could also contain elements of less light-hearted sentiments.

The introduction to the overture of *Don Giovanni* begins with the music that later announces the arrival of the Commendatore's statue in the second act, which culminates in the hero's demise. The end of the introduction follows uninterruptedly into the main allegro; the repeated notes in the strings remain constant, yet transform the character of the music. In the introduction they may seem to represent agitation or anguish, but as soon as they move from the violas and second violins to the celli, marking the end of the andante, the gravity of the introduction is instantly transformed into an open allegro. Although the speed of the repeated notes remains unchanged, the tempo is quadrupled and the harmony moves into major.

Don Giovanni is the perfect example of how a *dramma giocoso* embodies the very essence of music. Throughout the opera the more the subjective situation of a character becomes tragic, the more comic is the objective situation, and vice versa. For instance, the catalogue aria of Leporello ("Madamina, il catalogo") in the first act, in which he recounts the endless (and probably unsuccessful) exploits of his master is extremely humorous for Leporello, but shockingly tragic for Elvira, who thus discovers Giovanni's unfaithfulness. The musical parallel of the dichotomy of subjective and objective situations on the stage can be found, among others, in the tempo changes. Often, as in the overture, the pulse does not change from one section to the next, but instead is either doubled or halved, creating the sense, throughout the constant transformations of character in the music, that the tragic exists within the comic and the playful within the serious. One could say that the meter remains objective while the music expresses the subjective views of the characters or of the composer himself.

Mozart has often been portrayed as a childlike—if not childish—but inspired genius whose God-given talent allowed him to pour forth works effortlessly, as if dictated by some divine power. The fact that he was a genius, however, and therefore able to compose faster than anyone else, must not obscure the complex thought processes that went into the creation of his music. In reality, he was a thoroughly and rigorously trained musician who also possessed a remarkable understanding of human nature and a formidable intellectual capacity. All this is evident in the development of the characters in his operas and in the unique fantasy that led him to create a highly individual harmonic world, which he carefully crafted, attending to the most minute details of instrumentation and orchestration. His use of clarinets and oboes is one example of the care taken to differentiate the orchestral sound. The oboes obviously have a more penetrating expressive sound, whereas the clarinets have a unique, mellow quality to their sound. There is not a single symphony that includes both oboes and clarinets (with the exception of his second version of

Symphony No. 40, which he later rewrote, adding clarinets), and only one concerto, the C minor Piano Concerto KV 491. It is significant, then, that Mozart found the clarinets to be the better partners for Elvira's entrance and her aria "Mi tradì quell'alma ingrata," while the oboes play the main woodwind role in Anna's arias. Did he see Elvira as a mellower character? Or did he find Anna's desperation better mirrored by the sound of the oboes?

Mozart's use of trombones is quite rare; only a handful of his works include them. Two prominent examples of these are the cemetery scene in *Don Giovanni*, in which the statue of the Commendatore invites him to dinner (followed by his arrival), and the Tuba mirum of the *Requiem*, where the trombone plays an equally important part as the solo singers. He was so precise on this issue that the theme in the beginning of the overture of *Don Giovanni* is presented without trombones. However, when the same theme returns near the end of the second act to announce the arrival of the Commendatore, the sustained chords include trombones, thus adding another dimension to the sound, making it not only louder but fuller and darker, befitting the entrance of a supernatural character. The theme undergoes a transformation through its orchestration, just as Giovanni himself is transformed by the Commendatore's death.

There are, in fact, two different Giovannis in the opera: the one who exists before the Commendatore's death and the one who is left with the consequences of murder afterward. The first Giovanni is practically non-existent, as the duel takes place in the first scene of the first act. This development, however, conditions all the successive events of the plot, and one must understand its complexity in order to follow the way the death has changed his relationships, his way of living and the course of his life. It is not that he was simply a murderer. One must feel the transformation that takes place in him after the murder despite the very brief period he has onstage beforehand. The central issue of the drama is how something so banal as a duel (as it was at that time) inevitably changes his life completely, as well as the lives of those around him. Giovanni is not essentially a diabolical character with sinister intentions, nor does he long for the fusion of Eros and death, a theme developed so thoroughly by Wagner from another perspective. Giovanni leads his life in every moment the way he pleases, in absolute sincerity, without considering the consequences.

The other characters, independent as they may be, revolve around him as if their existence were meaningless without his presence. They are not merely satellites trapped in orbit around a far grander being, though; they are autonomous personalities, each one touched, in his own way, by the death of the Commendatore. In my opinion it is no coincidence that Mozart did not write a grand aria for Giovanni. It is his way of saying that he is not the only meaningful person on the stage. An aria affords an operatic figure the opportunity to share his most intimate emotions and anxieties, and this privilege is granted to all the victims of Giovanni's impulsiveness: Anna, Elvira, Ottavio, Zerlina and Leporello. Giovanni's psychological development must therefore be inferred solely from his interactions with the other characters in ensembles and recitatives.

Shortly after the murder, in a telling revelation of its impact on him, Giovanni forbids Leporello to speak of the Commendatore: *"purché non parli del Commendatore"* (*We'll leave the Commendatore out of it*) (– Act I, Scene 4, recitative). This particular death, and the subject of death in general, are taboo in his world. Giovanni senses that something completely out of the ordinary has transpired and he cannot measure the degree to which it will radically change his destiny. Nevertheless, at the end of the first act he remains impenitent, remorseless and arrogant: *"Ma non manca a me coraggio"* (*I'll never lack courage*). He is certain that terrestrial justice is powerless over him. Until the statue of the Commendatore appears in the second act this proves to be true and the plot remains realistic, based on human actions and human nature.

With the Commendatore, however, Mozart introduces a higher justice, a sudden metaphysical dimension, which returns us to the moment of the murder in the beginning of the opera. At this point the cyclical nature of the drama becomes clear, and we see that this, the introduction of divine justice, was already inherent in the murder itself and that the drama has been propelled to this moment with the inevitability of the Commendatore's theme with its relentless dotted rhythms.

In order to capture the deeper sense of this seemingly bizarre dramatic construction, one must regard the entire opera first through the eyes of Giovanni, then through those of Leporello and finally from Ottavio's point of view. Ottavio, who is often portrayed as a somewhat ambiguous, if not weak, character, is in fact not the least bit ridiculous and the proof lies in the importance of the music Mozart writes for him. Perhaps Ottavio is a friend of Giovanni's, may be even an intimate friend. It is not explicitly described this way in the score, but I find it highly probable. The fact that Giovanni seduces a peasant woman like Zerlina is not disconcerting to him; among aristocrats, this is perfectly acceptable behavior. To do the same with a woman of his own class, however, no less than Ottavio's fiancée, is truly disturbing, and to murder her father in the process, even if unintentionally, unforgivable; Giovanni breaks the unwritten rules of the cavalier, and now appears to Ottavio a blasphemous individual, one who disregards moral principles and norms.

How far the physical contact went between Giovanni and Anna is immaterial, and speculations of this nature are too base for the subject at hand: namely, that Giovanni awakens feelings in Anna previously unknown to her. Mozart's only musical insinuation as to what may have taken place between them is the way in which Anna describes the encounter to Ottavio. At the end of her *"Entrar io vidi in un mantello avvolto un uom"* (*A man comes in, wrapped in a cloak*—Act I, Scene 13, recitative), the orchestra holds a very sustained chord, after which there is a breathless moment of silence, followed by "*che al primo istante avea preso per voi*" (*for a second, dear friend, I thought it was you*). The music tells us that Ottavio would prefer not to know any more than Anna wants to tell him. "*Da lui mi sciolsi*" (*At last he released me*), Anna then says, confessing an embrace. Nevertheless, poor Ottavio replies, "*Ohimè, respiro*" (*Oh dear, I can breathe again*)—he seems relieved by her explanation. As I see it, his exhalation symbolizes his acceptance of whatever has happened and his contentedness with her love alone. As long as her fleeting passion for Giovanni has not interfered with her devotion to him, he is magnanimous enough to overlook a surreptitious embrace and convince himself to accept her rather dubious narration.

If Ottavio is often wrongly portrayed as a sheepish and humiliated lover, Elvira can be equally misunderstood as an obsessive and hysterical woman who is unable to get over Giovanni's rejection of her. When we look more closely, however, we notice her effect on him as a woman still so powerfully attractive that he is able to recognize her scent: "*Zitto: mi pare sentire odor di femmina*" (*Hush, I smell the sweet scent of a woman*— Act I, Scene 4, recitative). This moment is portrayed in many productions as commonplace, but is actually an allusion to the fact that their relationship is not entirely over. Elvira, far more than just an infatuated ex-lover, remains a magnet for Giovanni. Mozart shows this above all through the modulations that take place in the orchestra while she sings. The modulations that support the melodic flow in "Mi tradì" often reveal aspects of a character that are not obvious in the libretto.

Just as the vocal melody alone represents but one aspect of a character's personality, a quartet or sextet in a Mozart opera is never simply a quartet or sextet. It is an opportunity for division into smaller groups and individuals, whereby the private and possibly subversive intentions or views of each member or smaller group may be revealed as an aside. Every single voice may be simultaneously saying something completely different. Despite

the different texts, though, there is a definite sense of organization, sometimes with main and subsidiary voices, sometimes with
combinations of a number of main voices and some subsidiary
ones. Mozart's operatic ensembles explore all the possible combinations inherent in the number of voices. A quintet, for example,
can consist of one unit made up of the five voices, or any of the
following combinations: 2+3; 4+1; 2+1+1+1; 2+2+1; or 3+1+1.
In each case the roles can be exchanged during the course of the
ensemble piece; the two voices singing together can begin to sing
different parts and their unity can be replaced by two other voices.
Mozart makes use of all of these possible combinations of the
ensemble in order to serve the development of the plot and give us
an insight into the individual position of each character and his or
her alliances.

It has been extremely interesting to be able to restudy and
rethink this piece with the same cast—with only one exception—
in two different productions. I had the good fortune to be able
musically completely to restudy this work in the old production of
the Staatsoper during our trip to Japan in October 2007, and it is
with great joy that we now embark on this new production.

Original article appeared in the program to Peter Mussbach's
production of Don Giovanni *in December 2007.*

8

On the West-Eastern Divan Orchestra

AUGUST 2006

The West-Eastern Divan Orchestra is a humanitarian idea. It became the most important thing in Edward Said's life, as it still is in mine, and through it our ideals will always live on. Our project may not change the world, but it is a step forward. It is an ongoing dialogue in which the universal, physical and metaphysical language of music links with the continuous dialogue that we have with young people and that young people have with each other.

We don't see ourselves as a political project, but rather as a forum where young people from Israel, Palestine and the Arab countries can express themselves freely and openly while at the same time hearing the narrative of the other. It is not necessarily a question of accepting the narrative of the other, let alone agreeing with it, but rather the indispensable need to accept its legitimacy. We believe in only two absolutely necessary political ideas:

> There is no military solution to the Israeli-Palestinian conflict.
> The destinies of the Israeli and Palestinian people are inextricably linked and the land that some call Greater Israel and others Palestine is a land for two peoples.

Music makes the West-Eastern Divan possible because it does not contain limited associations as words do. Music teaches us that there is nothing that does not include its parallel or opposite as the case may be; therefore no element is entirely independent because the relationship is by definition interdependent. It is my belief that although music cannot solve any problems, since it is, as Busoni said, "sonorous air," it can teach us to think in a way that is a school for life. In music we know and accept the hierarchy of a main subject, we accept the permanent presence of an opposite and sometimes even of subversive accompanying rhythms.

The Sovereign Independent Republic of the West-Eastern Divan, as I like to call it, believes that if any progress is to be made in the Israeli-Palestinian dispute, it will require both sides to exercise sensitive speech and painful listening. Many of its citizens are hearing the painfulness of the other side for the first time and that is inevitably a shock that also requires them to think about the past and the suffering that has lasted for so many years.

I have come to believe that morality and strategy are not exclusive of each other, but rather go hand in hand in this conflict. If the two narratives are legitimate, their destinies inseparable, and there is no military solution, then the acceptance of the narrative of the other must inevitably lead to the logical conclusion that what is good for the one is in the long term good for the other. Is this a moral conclusion or a strategic one? I am convinced it is both.

Israel undoubtedly has a right to exist. The Palestinian people undoubtedly have a right to a sovereign, legitimate state. Israel needs security. The Palestinians need equality and dignity. Only they can provide that to each other. The Israeli army is very strong but unable to give the Israelis the security they want. Israel's security can, in the long term, come only through its acceptance by the Palestinians and other neighbors. At the moment, the Palestinians, equality and dignity can be provided only by Israel. Occupation of land is a hindrance and its end long overdue. Unilateral decisions have proved to be disastrous. Only honest and courageous negotiations between parties, directly or indirectly connected, can lead to conditions that will be liveable both for the Israelis and the Palestinians. Isolation of parties will make them part of the problem; inclusion will make them part of the solution. I have frequently been admired for certain initiatives, often with the added allusion to naïveté on my part. Isn't the reliance on a military solution that has not worked for sixty years even more naïve?

Our project is very much in opposition to the cruelty and savagery that has denied so many innocent civilians the possibility to continue living, fulfilling their ideas and dreams. It also shows me that so many lessons of the past have either been forgotten or never understood. Time not only helps define content, but influences it directly. How long will it take for people in the region to accept this and remember that the past is but a transition to the present and the present a transition to the future? Therefore, a violent and cruel present will inevitably lead to an even more cruel and violent future.

Every member of this orchestra, regardless of his or her origin, shows a remarkable amount of courage, understanding and vision by coming here. I would like to think of them as pioneers in a new way of thinking for the Middle East.

Original article published in Le Monde.

9

On Mozart

27 JANUARY 2006

Maestro, have you dreamt of Mozart?

No, should I?

Maybe. You've concentrated on his work so often—as a pianist, as a conductor. That certainly must be quite an intense relationship.

It is quite intense, but I don't think I've ever dreamt of a composer. Sometimes I dream about a certain piece, but I've never dreamt about a composer as a person or a historical figure.

Do you sometimes yearn to return to Mozart when you're working on entirely different music?

I wouldn't put it that way, for that would pit Mozart against other composers. That wouldn't do justice either to him or to the others. But I am certainly very happy and grateful that Mozart has accompanied me all my life. I personally don't need any Mozart years, because for me there isn't a single year without Mozart. And if I could choose a composer from the past to spend twenty-four hours with, it would of course be Mozart. Twenty-four hours of Mozart: that's like a whole week of living. Twenty-four hours with Mozart, that's like a month with Brahms—and nothing against Brahms.

Do you mean that in a musical sense? Is Mozart faster, does he have more to say with fewer notes?

There you go making judgments again! What's always fascinated me about Mozart's music is its special mix of depth and lightness. That is what makes him so difficult to play, conduct, or sing. For in the very moment that you focus on this or that aspect and say, I'd like to emphasize this, it's already over. Already there's nothing left. There's no other composer where each contour is so strongly defined by its opposite. That's why the Da Ponte operas are the ultimate for me: take *Don Giovanni*, a *dramma giocoso*. That means if the subjective situation is tragic—as in Donna Anna's case—the objective situation is comic and the other way round. Mozart is the most comprehensive of all composers. In Mozart the comic is only to be had with something dark; the dark is never without its comic aspect.

That sounds like a lesson for life.

That is a lesson for life! And for me that's even true in a literal sense. I played my first Mozart piano concerto when I was eight years old. And just imagine, last year I first really discovered the piano trios. Unbelievable pieces! And anyway, I think in general that we allow ourselves to learn something from music for life, and not just the other way around.

Does the "child prodigy" Daniel Barenboim feel a connection to the child prodigy Wolfgang Amadeus Mozart?

In a certain sense, yes. Look, I know very well what it means always to be too young for everything. For a very esteemed jury at Rome's Accademia di Santa Cecilia I once played Beethoven's Sonata Op. 111 . . .

. . . the opus summum of the piano literature . . .

I was thirteen then. Years later, Arturo Benedetti Michelangeli, a great pianist who sat on the jury, took me aside and told me that I had received nine yes votes and one no vote—and the no vote was from him. The reason: he said a child couldn't know where to begin in the face of that music. So I was permanently confronted with the fact that one needs to have a great life experience to be a good musician. That is, of course, true. There are certain things you can only learn later in life.

Sensuality, for example, and of course that has an impact on your feeling for sound. But you can also learn a lot from music for life. We just don't do it.

Was Mozart able to do that? It's often claimed that he didn't have to or couldn't develop because he was so far ahead of the game.

If there's something that we can learn from Mozart today, then it's not to take everything so seriously. Every situation, no matter how tragic or horrible, has a light side. I learned that from Mozart. It's all a question of keeping things in proportion. In Wagner, we speak of space and time. In Mozart, you need to speak of content and its speed. What can be immediately understood about Mozart's music is that certain things need a lot of time, while others have to be done immediately and tolerate no delay.

How did Mozart know that?

That I can't tell you, it's been a few days since I last talked to him. (*Laughs.*) But let me clarify once more: Wagner sympathizes with the person who takes himself and his thoughts enormously seriously—in the end, he took himself very seriously as well. Mozart, in contrast, says that nothing in life is inherently moral, immoral, amoral, unless the human being makes something moral, immoral, or amoral out of it.

So everything's my own fault?

I wouldn't put it in such "moralistic" terms. I am responsible for myself, that's what Mozart shows me.

Can Mozart be hated, just like Wagner has sometimes been hated— and still can be hated today?

No, but there are surely people who think Mozart is overrated. That's a question of the *zeitgeist*. Isaac Albéniz, for example, a passionate Wagnerian, said that when he was very young he wrote in a letter how horribly he was bored by a performance of *Così fan tutte*—conducted by Richard Strauss! No one would dare say that today. Maybe people think it, but nobody says it aloud. Mozart is a fixed part of our canon. He is never questioned in his achievement—but that's something that can also be a problem.

Do you know of any boring, irrelevant, bad pieces by Mozart?

That's all relative. Compared to other composers with his own contemporaries, say—no. Compared with his best pieces, the Da Ponte operas, as I said, or the piano concertos—sure. Now this is very subjective, but playing the Coronation Concerto, K 587, gives me an incomparable physical pleasure in the fingers. But of course I know that this concerto in its slow movement doesn't have the depth of Concerto K 595. There are Mozart compositions that don't have everything.

What Mozart performers or conductors do you especially admire?

The pianists Edwin Fischer and Clifford Curzon. And yes, Wilhelm Furtwängler, whom I heard as an eleven-year-old in Salzburg conducting *Don Giovanni*. Whereby in his case, of course, not everything about his opera interpretations was convincing. The G minor symphony under Furtwängler: that is for me still today one of the greatest.

Does Furtwängler, the tragedian, lack something of the necessary lightness? Do Germans in general have a hard time with Mozart?

Maybe Furtwängler lacked a bit of humor, sure. It's paradoxical: the Germans accept the Italian Mozart just as little as the Italians want to take notice of the German Mozart. And the music is always both. Bach, for example, was thoroughly German, as was Brahms at any event, and Weber and Wagner as well—Schubert was Austrian through and through. Mozart was the first pan-European. He spoke many languages, German, Italian and French. He wrote operas in two languages and songs in French. Mozart and Liszt are the only two true Europeans. That was and still is something that really interests me personally.

Because this cosmopolitan aspect corresponds in a certain way to your own biography?

Probably. Living with several identities is something that I'm quite familiar with. That doesn't mean that everything is just as

close to me. In *The Magic Flute*, for example, to stick with
Mozart, I lack the *italianità*. That's why I've always had such a
problem with this opera.

*Has there been something like a key Mozart experience in your artistic
life? A piece, a moment when you suddenly felt you truly understood
Mozart?*

I gave my debut concert in London with the conductor Josef
Krips when I was thirteen. On the program was Mozart's
Concerto in A major. At a rehearsal Krips said to me, if you
play it that way, it sounds like Beethoven. Beethoven isn't
Mozart. Beethoven strives toward heaven and Mozart is from
heaven. That might be a bit over the top—imagine, he said that
in English, with a Vienna accent!—but it's right. You make
certain associations with Mozart—that was already true for me
as a child. Humor, death, suffering. One doesn't think so much
of repression or everything authoritarian. But when confronted
with the finale from the second act of *Figaro*, with the
benevolent fascism of the Count, then you suddenly discover
this aspect as well.

*It is said that in Mozart's operas the libretto often lies, but the music
always tells the truth. Is that right?*

I think so. That's why I find it so hard to bear all these
directing experiments in the case of the *Così fan tutte* finale. The
music is so easy, so self-evident, in a radiant C major. And
directors tear their hair out over this, the question of how to
how break this finale; there are whole philosophies built up
around this.

*At least the opera deals with true and false feelings, fidelity and
betrayal. Fiordiligi, Dorabella, Guglielmo and Ferrando have just
changed partners, can you just go on as if nothing had happened?*

But that's the wrong question! I recently argued for hours
about that with director Patrice Chéreau. Maybe it's because
Da Ponte wrote this libretto entirely on his own and couldn't,
as in *Figaro*, lean on Beaumarchais. At any event, *Così* is not as

well put together. The whole thing is not a tragic relationship drama that reveals at the end its truth and the depth of the fall. Mozart just shows that feelings are fragile. I love you—but I love you as well. That's possible, it happens in real life too. And it has nothing at all to do with our current *zeitgeist* or promiscuity, nothing. You diminish the piece if you bring it up to date.

Many of your fellow conductors—Harnoncourt, Gardiner, Jacobs Minkowski—found their way to Mozart from Baroque music and historical performance practice. And they have molded the current Mozart image—Mozart the rhetorician, the speaker of tones. You come declaredly not from this direction. Do you feel a bit alone?

To be quite frank, I couldn't care less. I have two problems with the so-called authentic performance practice movement. First of all, the fact that it's a movement at all, an ideology, a worldview, that asks fewer questions, but rather knows the right answers from the get go. That puts a limit on human creativity. That doesn't mean there aren't many unbelievably talented, fabulous musicians among my early performance practice colleagues. But the movement has in a sense broken out individual elements from the music—sound, tempo—as if they were independent of one another. I think that's a huge nonsense. Second, and I say this without any irony, this ideology has been able to sell itself as progressive. That's why it's so successful, that was its greatest triumph. I ask you: what can be progressive about saying let's look back at the way things were?!

Because it allows us to expand our hearing, disciplining and schooling our perception?

Of course you can learn a lot. It's also not as if everyone else still performs Mozart as was the case in Karajan's day, with fourteen first violins in the Berlin Philharmonic. As I started out in the 1970s working with the English Chamber Orchestra, we naturally oriented ourselves to the findings of the most recent Bärenreiter edition, and I had just six first violins. By the way, I always like to recall a letter Mozart wrote to his father from Mannheim: how happy he was to present his C major Symphony with twenty first violinists—and that in a small hall! And today people want to tell me that the only stylistically correct way is to appear with four violins in the Philharmonie? That's idiotic.

But didn't the use of modern means lead to a thickening of Mozart, a sweetening, at least making him sound like Brahms? The lazy, comfortable tempi, the big vibrato . . .

Vibrato, vibrato! What's the use of preaching the virtue of gut strings if the singers use vibrato as always? No, the question is, how can we use today's means in a responsible fashion. Of course our ears are also familiar with Stravinsky's *Rite of Spring*, of course we are used to dynamics having endlessly many shades and nuances from Tchaikovsky. That's decidedly not the case in Mozart. In terms of dynamics, Mozart is more black and white. If a phrase begins in piano, then it stays more or less piano, even if a huge expressive moment comes up in the middle. As a conductor, the question I need to ask is: what is the musical reason for this dynamic? And: how do I shape the phrase without on the one hand moving to a huge forte like Tchaikovsky, but at the same time without letting it go by without any expression at all? The current Mozart reception is between these two poles—very narrow, very small.

Maybe we can agree that today we want to be able to hear from the articulation, from the dynamics, whether Mozart or Tchaikovsky is at issue.

I don't know if that's enough. Just recently a young orchestra player came to me saying, "You can't play Beethoven like that any more!" That is the attitude that I meant: our civilization today is weaker, thinner; because we no longer have the courage to ask our own questions. We think in answers—and, even worse, other people's answers. Young people can't do anything about it: they grew up with it. I would expand the whole thing even to today's concept of democracy, this horrible political correctness that so marks Western society: the people can do anything they want, but they don't trust themselves to think independently. Seen that way, a dictatorship—regardless whether right or left—is surely more productive, creative. I know what's forbidden, so I try to find out how I can still do what I want.

Is there something that can't be done with Mozart?

You can't exaggerate or underline things. In Beethoven that works; I can focus so much on a particular place, even neglecting the rest. Of course, I always have to look what just happened and what follows, but still. Mozart doesn't know of such priorities. To that extent his music is a really impressive model for democratic living: everything is integrated into it. The leading voice and the secondary voice always both have something to say. In the piano sonatas, for example, there is not one place where the right hand plays the melody and the left hand just goes du-di-da-di-du-di. In Mozart, there's always someone opposite, a commentary, a second person.

That sounds very comforting. But why then is Mozart so difficult for us today?

Because we lack the culture. That's true of directors just as it is of pianists or conductors. We know too much that isn't important for him. And that has nothing to do with encyclopedic knowledge. Edwin Fischer once put it nicely: Mozart is the heart's touchstone. That's right.

Mozart, the distant, the difficult?

Oh, Mozart has always been misunderstood. Take, for example, his last piano concerto, B flat major K 595, premiered in the year of his death in Vienna. Do you know when the piece was played the next time? In 1929, by Artur Schnabel, again in Vienna! If you look back at which of the great composers engaged with Mozart, Wagner didn't, Brahms neither. The only one before Richard Strauss was really Franz Liszt. That means, those who don't swim with the current of the time can sometimes see more.

Mozart, the provocateur?

I do think that he provokes us, simply because it is much easier to identify with the greatness, the courage of a Beethoven or the sensuality, the freedom of a Wagner, anarchy is always erotic, if you like, because you can always be relatively sure that the insistence on it in art has very little to do with real life. But Mozart says, greatness, sensuality, but what else? Mozart points at us, at you and me. And has a much deeper, much broader understanding of human nature than we can come up with today. That's what makes him so strange to us.

Interview with Christine Lemke-Matwey, translated by Brian Currid.

10

On Dual Citizenship

I have often made the statement that the destinies of the Israeli and Palestinian peoples are inextricably linked and that there is no military solution to the conflict. My recent acceptance of Palestinian nationality has given me the opportunity to demonstrate this more tangibly. When my family moved to Israel from Argentina in the 1950s, one of my parents' intentions was to spare me the experience of growing up as part of a minority—a Jewish minority. They wanted to me to grow up as part of a majority—a Jewish majority. The tragedy of this is that my generation, despite having been educated in a society whose positive aspects and human values have greatly enriched my thinking, ignored the existence of a minority within Israel—a non-Jewish minority—which had been the majority in the whole of Palestine until the creation of the state of Israel in 1948. Part of the non-Jewish population remained in Israel and other parts left out of fear or were forcefully displaced.

In the Israeli-Palestinian conflict there was and still is an inability to admit the interdependence of their two voices. The creation of the state of Israel was the result of a Jewish-European idea, which, if it is to extend its leitmotif into the future, must accept the Palestinian identity as an equally valid leitmotif. The demographic development is impossible to ignore; the Palestinians within Israel are a minority but a rapidly growing one and their voice needs to be heard now more than ever. Currently they make up approximately 22 percent of the population of Israel. This is a larger percentage than was ever represented by a Jewish minority in any country in any period of history. The total number of Palestinians living within Israel and in the occupied territories (that is, greater Israel for the Israelis or greater Palestine for the Palestinians) is already larger than the Jewish population.

At present, Israel is confronted at once with three problems: the nature of the modern democratic Jewish state (its very identity); the problem of Palestinian identity within Israel; *and* the problem of the creation of a Palestinian state outside Israel. With Jordan and Egypt it was possible to attain what can best be described as an ice-cold peace without questioning Israel's existence as a Jewish state. The problem of the Palestinians within Israel, however, is a much more challenging one to solve, both theoretically and practically. For Israel it means, among other things, coming to terms with the fact that the land was not barren or empty, "a land without a people," an idea that was propagated at the time of its creation. For the Palestinians it means accepting the fact that Israel is a Jewish state and is here to stay.

Israelis, however, must accept the integration of the Palestinian minority even if it means changing certain aspects of the nature of Israel; they must also accept the justification for and necessity of the creation of a Palestinian state next to the state of Israel. Not only is there no alternative, or magic wand, that will make the Palestinians disappear, but their integration is an indispensable condition—on moral, social and political grounds—for the very survival of Israel. The longer the occupation continues and Palestinian dissatisfaction remains unaddressed, the more difficult it is to find even elementary common ground. We have seen so often in the modern history of the Middle East that missed opportunities for reconciliation have had extremely negative results for both sides.

For my part, when the Palestinian passport was offered to me, I accepted it in the spirit of acknowledging the Palestinian destiny which I, as an Israeli, share. A true citizen of Israel must reach out to the Palestinian people with openness and at the very least an attempt to understand what the creation of the state of Israel has meant to them. The day of Independence for the Jews, May 15, 1948, is *Al Nakba*, the catastrophe, for the Palestinians. A true citizen of Israel must ask himself what the Jews, known as an intelligent people of learning and culture, have done to share their cultural heritage with the Palestinians. A true citizen of Israel must also ask himself why the Palestinians have been condemned to live in slums and accept lower standards of education and medical care, rather than being provided by the occupying force with decent, dignified and liveable conditions, a right common to all human beings.

In any occupied territory the occupiers are responsible for the quality of life of the occupied and, in the case of the Palestinians, the different Israeli governments over the last forty years have failed miserably. The Palestinians naturally must continue to resist the occupation and all attempts to deny them basic individual needs and statehood. However, for their own sake this resistance must not express itself through violence. Crossing the boundary from adamant resistance (including non-violent demonstrations and protests) to violence only results in more innocent victims and does not serve the long-term interests of the Palestinian people. At the same time, the citizens of Israel have just as much cause to be alert to the needs and rights of the Palestinian people (both within and outside Israel) as they do to their own. After all, in the sense that we share one land and one destiny, we should all have dual citizenship.

Notes

Chapter 1

1 Aristotle, *Politics*, Book 8, Section V.
2 Beethoven, Piano Sonata Op. 13, bars 1–2.
3 Wagner, *Tristan und Isolde*, Prelude, bars 1–3.
4 Beethoven, Piano Sonata Op. 109, bars 1–8.
5 From *Die Musik in Geschichte und Gegenwart, allgemeine Enzyklopädie der Musik bergründet von Friedrich Blume*, Bärenreiter edition.

Chapter 2

1 Beethoven, Symphony No. 5, first movement, bars 1–5; bars 240–52.
2 Beethoven, *Diabelli Variations*: theme, bars 1–8, variation, bars 1–8.
3 *Wagner on Music and Drama*, arranged by Albert Goldman and Evert Sprinchorn, Victor Gollancz, London, 1970, p. 365.
4 Thomas Mann, *The Magic Mountain*, translated by H. T. Lowe-Porter, Vintage Books, New York, 1999, pp. 111, 112.

Chapter 4

1 Beethoven, Piano Sonata Op. 13, third movement (Adagio Cantabile), bars 1–8.
2 Bach, *Well-Tempered Clavier*, Book 1, Prelude 24 in B minor, bars 1–7.
3 Schoenberg, Variations for Orchestra, Op. 31, first variation, bars 1–3.

Chapter 6

1 Paul Mendes-Flohr (ed.), *A Land of Two Peoples: Martin Buber on Jews and Arabs*, University of Chicago Press, Chicago, 2005.

Index